Biography Today

*Profiles
of People
of Interest
to Young
Readers*

Volume 13
Issue 2
April 2004

Cherie D. Abbey
Managing Editor

Kevin Hillstrom
Editor

*615 Griswold Street
Detroit, Michigan 48͵*

D1468251

Cherie D. Abbey, *Managing Editor*
Kevin Hillstrom, *Editor*

Peggy Daniels, Leif Gruenberg, Laurie Lanzen Harris, Jeff Hill,
Laurie Hillstrom, Sara Pendergast, Tom Pendergast, Diane Telgen,
Sue Ellen Thompson, Matt Totsky, and Rhoda Wilburn, *Sketch Writers*

Barry Puckett, *Research Associate*

Allison A. Beckett, Mary Butler, and Linda Strand, *Research Assistants*

Omnigraphics, Inc.

* * *

Matthew P. Barbour, *Senior Vice President*
Kay Gill, *Vice President — Directories*
Kevin Hayes, *Operations Manager*
Leif Gruenberg, *Development Manager*
David P. Bianco, *Marketing Manager*

* * *

Peter E. Ruffner, *Publisher*
Frederick G. Ruffner, Jr., *Chairman*

Copyright © 2004 Omnigraphics, Inc.
ISSN 1058-2347 • ISBN 0-7808-0682-4

This book is printed on acid-free paper meeting the ANSI Z39.48 Standard. The infinity symbol that appears above indicates that the paper in this book meets that standard.

Printed in the United States

INDEXED IN
Children's Magazine Guide

Contents

Preface

Biography Today is a magazine designed and written for the young reader—ages 9 and above—and covers individuals that librarians and teachers tell us that young people want to know about most: entertainers, athletes, writers, illustrators, cartoonists, and political leaders.

The Plan of the Work

The publication was especially created to appeal to young readers in a format they can enjoy reading and readily understand. Each issue contains approximately 10 sketches arranged alphabetically. Each entry provides at least one picture of the individual profiled, and bold-faced rubrics lead the reader to information on birth, youth, early memories, education, first jobs, marriage and family, career highlights, memorable experiences, hobbies, and honors and awards. Each of the entries ends with a list of easily accessible sources designed to lead the student to further reading on the individual and a current address. Obituary entries are also included, written to provide a perspective on the individual's entire career. Obituaries are clearly marked in both the table of contents and at the beginning of the entry.

Biographies are prepared by Omnigraphics editors after extensive research, utilizing the most current materials available. Those sources that are generally available to students appear in the list of further reading at the end of the sketch.

Indexes

A new index now appears in all *Biography Today* publications. In an effort to make the index easier to use, we have combined the **Name** and **General Index** into one, called the **Cumulative Index**. This new index contains the names of all individuals who have appeared in *Biography Today* since the series began. The names appear in bold faced type, followed by the issue in which they appeared. The General Index also contains the occupations, nationalities, and ethnic and minority origins of individuals profiled. The General Index is cumulative, including references to all individuals who have appeared in the *Biography Today* General Series and the *Biography Today* Special Subject volumes since the series began in 1992.

In a further effort to consolidate and save space, the Birthday and Places of Birth Indexes will be appearing only in the September issue and in the Annual Cumulation.

Our Advisors

This series was reviewed by an Advisory Board comprised of librarians, children's literature specialists, and reading instructors to ensure that the concept of this publication — to provide a readable and accessible biographical magazine for young readers — was on target. They evaluated the title as it developed, and their suggestions have proved invaluable. Any errors, however, are ours alone. We'd like to list the Advisory Board members, and to thank them for their efforts.

Sandra Arden, *Retired*
Assistant Director
Troy Public Library, Troy, MI

Gail Beaver
University of Michigan School of Information
Ann Arbor, MI

Marilyn Bethel, *Retired*
Broward County Public Library System
Fort Lauderdale, FL

Nancy Bryant
Brookside School Library,
Cranbrook Educational Community
Bloomfield Hills, MI

Cindy Cares
Southfield Public Library
Southfield, MI

Linda Carpino
Detroit Public Library
Detroit, MI

Carol Doll
Wayne State University Library and Information Science Program
Detroit, MI

Helen Gregory
Grosse Pointe Public Library
Grosse Pointe, MI

Jane Klasing, *Retired*
School Board of Broward County
Fort Lauderdale, FL

Marlene Lee
Broward County Public Library System
Fort Lauderdale, FL

Sylvia Mavrogenes
Miami-Dade Public Library System
Miami, FL

Carole J. McCollough
Detroit, MI

Rosemary Orlando
St. Clair Shores Public Library
St. Clair Shores, MI

Renee Schwartz
Broward County Public Library System
Fort Lauderdale, FL

Lee Sprince
Broward West Regional Library
Fort Lauderdale, FL

Susan Stewart, *Retired*
Birney Middle School Reading
Laboratory, Southfield, MI

Ethel Stoloff, *Retired*
Birney Middle School Library
Southfield, MI

Our Advisory Board stressed to us that we should not shy away from controversial or unconventional people in our profiles, and we have tried to follow their advice. The Advisory Board also mentioned that the sketches might be useful in reluctant reader and adult literacy programs, and we would value any comments librarians might have about the suitability of our magazine for those purposes.

Your Comments Are Welcome

Our goal is to be accurate and up-to-date, to give young readers information they can learn from and enjoy. Now we want to know what you think. Take a look at this issue of *Biography Today*, on approval. Write or call me with your comments. We want to provide an excellent source of biographical information for young people. Let us know how you think we're doing.

Cherie Abbey
Managing Editor, *Biography Today*
Omnigraphics, Inc.
615 Griswold Street
Detroit, MI 48226

editor@biographytoday.com
www.biographytoday.com

Congratulations!

Congratulations to the following individuals and libraries, who are receiving a free copy of *Biography Today*, Vol. 13, No. 2 for suggesting people who appear in this issue:

Leigh Jordon, Lancaster, SC
Rose M. Rivas, San Antonio, TX
Sheron Rundall, Dallas, GA

Tony Blair 1953-
British Political Leader
Prime Minister of the United Kingdom

BIRTH

Anthony Charles Lynton Blair was born on May 6, 1953, in Edinburgh, Scotland. He was the second child born to Leo Blair, a lawyer and university professor, and Hazel (Corscaden) Blair, a homemaker. He has an older brother, William, and a younger sister, Sarah.

YOUTH

Shortly after Tony was born, the Blairs moved with their two sons to Glasgow, Scotland, where Leo Blair worked as a tax inspector while studying for a law degree. In 1954 they moved again, this time all the way to southern Australia, where Leo had been hired to teach law at the University of Adelaide. Still wearing diapers, Tony entertained the other passengers on the long boat trip to Australia with his dancing. His younger sister Sarah was born in Adelaide, while Tony attended pre-school and continued to show a flair for performing in public.

The Blairs returned to England after three years, settling in the northern city of Durham. There, Leo Blair taught law at the University of Durham and got involved in local politics. In 1963 he ran for Parliament (see box on pages 15 and 16) as a member of the Conservative party, but during the campaign he suffered a serious stroke. Tony was only 11 at the time, but he remembers this event as "the day my childhood ended." "My father was a very ambitious man," he later told his biographer, John Rentoul. "He was successful. He was a go-getter. One morning I woke to be told that he had had a stroke in the middle of the night and might not live through the day and my whole world then fell apart." But, he goes on to explain, "It taught me something. It taught me the value of the family, because my mother worked for three years to help him talk and walk again. But it taught me something else, too. When that happened, the fairweather friends — they went. That's not unusual. But the real friends, the true friends, they stayed with us. They helped us, and they stuck with us for no other reason than that it was the right thing to do." Years later, when Blair was running for public office and was accused of having led a privileged life as a child, he would often refer back to this experience and how it taught him to value loyalty and a clear sense of right and wrong. He would also mention how his father's sudden change from a young, healthy man to a bedridden one made him more

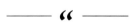

> *Blair remembers the day his father had a stroke as "the day my childhood ended." "My father was a very ambitious man," he later said. "He was successful. He was a go-getter. One morning I woke to be told that he had had a stroke in the middle of the night and might not live through the day and my whole world then fell apart."*

aware of "the changes that can happen overnight and the fact that you can go down as well as up in the world."

Leo Blair was only 40 at the time of his stroke, and he was eventually able to resume work as a lawyer. But his political career was over. The family was just beginning to adjust to his new situation when Tony's younger sister, Sarah, developed a form of rheumatoid arthritis. "My sister was in the hospital for two years, as they treated the illness quite differently then," Blair said. "It was a terrible thing because she had to have all sorts of drugs. My mum was coping with that and my dad at the same time and she was an absolute rock. I didn't see her break down, never once." Sarah's illness, combined with Leo Blair's slow recovery, caused severe emotional and financial stress for the family. But once again, this difficult period instilled in young Tony some of the qualities that would later account for his success. He learned the value of hard work and responsibility, he came to admire his mother's ability to bear up under an enormous amount of strain, and he would eventually prove that he had inherited his father's political ambition.

"It taught me the value of the family," Blair said about his father's stroke, "because my mother worked for three years to help him talk and walk again. But it taught me something else, too. When that happened, the fairweather friends — they went. That's not unusual. But the real friends, the true friends, they stayed with us. They helped us, and they stuck with us for no other reason than that it was the right thing to do."

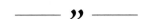

EDUCATION

After spending his early years at a "pre-prep" school called Western Hill, Tony enrolled in the Durham Choristers School as a day student at age eight. This was a private school — which in England is referred to as "public." In addition to his studies, he played cricket and rugby and performed in school plays. He was often referred to as "Blair Two" because his older brother, William, also attended the school. Although he was considered smart enough to skip a grade, Tony was primarily interested in sports.

It is common for children from middle- and upper-class British families to be sent off to boarding school in their early teens. At age 13, Tony went to

Blair with his parents and brother in 1956.

Fettes College in Edinburgh, the city in Scotland where he had been born. Fettes was the most prestigious private secondary school in Scotland, and it was often described as the Scottish version of Eton, the well-known English boarding school where upper-class and even royal families send their sons. Although he claims he "did not shine at anything" during his years at Fettes, he played basketball and rugby and was captain of the cricket team (a game that combines elements of baseball and croquet). He also displayed a rebellious streak, particularly when it came to rules that he thought were unfair. Fettes encouraged the tradition known in England as "fagging," where younger boys are forced to run errands and perform menial chores for older boys, who beat them with a cane if they don't do their jobs right. Tony hated this custom, and at the beginning of his second year at Fettes he tried to run away. He was forced to return to school, but these were not the happiest years of his life.

After graduating from Fettes in 1971, Tony took what is commonly referred to as a "gap year," which is a year off between high school and college. He spent it in London, hauling musical equipment around the city for rock bands in an old van. He and a friend thought they could set up a business promoting and managing rock bands, and Tony spent much of his time handing out leaflets and trying to book performances for a band called Jaded. But he was unable to support himself on his earnings, so he had to take on a number of odd jobs as well. After sleeping on sofas in his friends' apartments for a year, he decided he was ready to go back to school and complete his education.

In 1972, Blair entered St. John's College at Oxford University, where he studied law. At that time, in the early 1970s, student protests against the Vietnam War were disrupting many college campuses. But Blair didn't get involved in campus politics or anti-war protests at Oxford. He grew his hair long, wore bell-bottom jeans and colorful shirts, and sang in a rock band called the Ugly Rumors, but he avoided the drug culture that was so prevalent on college campuses at the time. Instead, he became very interested in religion, especially after making friends with Peter Thomson, an Oxford classmate who was studying theology. Thomson introduced Blair to the teachings of Scottish philosopher John Macmurray, who believed that people should work for the benefit of the community rather than to meet their own individual needs. Blair was deeply affected by Macmurray's ideas. "My Christianity and my politics came together at the same time," he recalls. He was confirmed in the Church of England at the end of his second year at Oxford, and he began thinking of ways that he could put his religious beliefs to work for the good of a larger community. Blair graduated from Oxford in 1975.

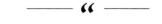

"She knew she was dying but she was very, very lucid," Blair said about his mother. "She saw each one of us in turn and went through things with us. . . . She was very keen as to what type of future life we should lead. . . . I was always the wildest of the three [and] Mum was worried I might go off the rails."

Two weeks after Blair graduated from Oxford, his mother died of throat cancer at the age of 52. Her death—much like his father's stroke 12 years earlier—had a profound effect on Blair. "She knew she was dying but she was very, very lucid," he recalled. "She saw each one of us in turn and went through things with us. . . . She was very keen as to what type of future life we should lead. . . . I was always the wildest of the three [and] Mum was worried I might go off the rails." Before she died, Hazel Blair made both her sons promise "that we'd get ourselves sorted out and not do stupid things."

Tony Blair suddenly realized that if there were things he wanted to accomplish in his life, he'd better not waste any more time. "My life took on an urgency that has probably never left it," he said. Planning to practice law, he immediately completed a one-year law course in preparation for the bar exam. He passed the bar in 1976.

CAREER HIGHLIGHTS

After completing his law studies, Blair began an unpaid apprenticeship — known as a "pupilage" — at a law firm run by Derry Irvine. Irvine had also taken on another pupil, Cherie Booth, who had graduated first in her class at the London School of Economics and would later become Blair's wife. Irvine could only choose one of his pupils for a "tenancy" or permanent job with the firm at the end of their year-long pupilage. Blair had performed only marginally on the bar exam while Booth had achieved one of the top scores, but it was Blair who was asked to join Irvine's firm. "One of his principal skills was absorbing enormously complicated material," Irvine recalls. "He had a very keen sense of what was relevant. He was very good at getting to the point . . . [and he possessed] an excellent facility with the English language."

Becoming a Member of Parliament

It was around this time that Blair began to get involved in the Labour party, one of Great Britain's two dominant political parties (see box on pages 15 and 16). The Labour party had traditionally been dominated by trade unions. But a series of strikes in the late 1970s seriously disrupted British life and commerce, and many people became disenchanted with the Labour party. Many Labour voters switched their support to Conservative party candidates in the election of 1979, when Margaret Thatcher became Prime Minister. In 1982, Blair decided to run for Parliament as a Labour candidate from Beaconsfield, a district west of London that had almost always voted Conservative. He won only 10 percent of the votes, but he made a very good impression on party leaders during his campaign. The following year he ran again, this time in Sedgefield, an industrial area near Durham, and won.

Once he became a Member of Parliament (MP), Blair proved himself to be a quick learner. While Margaret Thatcher and the Conservatives continued to run the government, Blair rose rapidly through the ranks of the Labour

*The Houses of Parliament at the Palace of Westminster,
with Big Ben shown at the right.*

Government in the United Kingdom

The United Kingdom consists of England, Scotland, Wales, and Northern Ireland. The U.K. has a parliamentary form of government, which means that the lawmaking body known as Parliament is the supreme authority. The Parliament consists of the *monarch* (currently Queen Elizabeth II), the *House of Commons,* and the *House of Lords.* The role of the monarch is largely ceremonial with no real power, and the term "Parliament" is often used to refer just to the two law-making bodies, the House of Commons and House of Lords. There is no written constitution that gives Parliament its authority. Its power has evolved over many centuries and is based not only on law, but also on custom and tradition. The two houses of Parliament meet in the Palace of Westminster, which is located in London next to the River Thames. The building has three sections, one for the House of Commons, one for the House of Lords, and a royal apartment for the monarch. Although still considered a Royal Palace, the last monarch to live here was Henry VIII, who moved out in 1512. The clock tower Big Ben is also part of the building.

The **House of Commons** has 659 members (known as *Members of Parliament* or MPs) who are elected by the voters, much the way Americans elect their senators and congressional representatives. There are currently two main political parties, the Conservative party (also known as Tories) and the Labour party. Whichever party wins the most seats in the House of Commons during a general election (see below) gets to choose its leader as the *Prime Minister*. For example, the Labour party won the most seats in the 2001 general election, so its leader, Tony Blair, became the Prime Minister. The main function of the House of Commons is to pass laws and to oversee "the Government."

In the U.K., "the Government" consists of the Prime Minister and about 100 members of the political party that is currently in power. These 100 members can be from either the House of Commons or the House of Lords. They work in government departments to manage public services.

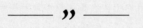

The Parliament consists of the **monarch** *(currently Queen Elizabeth II), the* **House of Commons,** *and the* **House of Lords.**

The **House of Lords** has approximately 700 members, known as peers, who are not elected. There are 500 *life peers*, who are appointed by the Queen on the recommendation of the Prime Minister and who have typically served the country in other capacities in the past. They hold their positions for life. This group includes about 12 *law lords* — high-ranking judges who act as a final court of appeal. There are 26 bishops or *lords spiritual* representing the Church of England, which is the official church of the British government. Finally, there are 92 *hereditary peers,* who have inherited their seats in Parliament from the families. These peers have traditionally been members of British nobility. The hereditary peers at one time dominated the House of Lords, but today their influence has been reduced, and most hold their position for life rather than passing it on to their children. The main function of the House of Lords is to review legislation passed by the House of Commons.

General elections must be held at least every five years. During that period of time, it is the Prime Minister's responsibility to call for a general election. A general election is also held when Parliament votes that it has "no confidence" in the Prime Minister and his cabinet, or when Parliament defeats a measure that the Prime Minister considers absolutely essential. When a general election is called for, the Prime Minister and all elected Members of Parliament lose their positions and must go home to campaign for them all over again

Blair (right) is shown working with fellow members of the Labour party in 1993.

party. In late 1984 he was promoted to the position known as "front bench," or spokesperson for treasury and economic affairs. Less than three years later he became his party's spokesperson on trade and industry. Just as the Conservatives had their cabinet ministers, the Labour party had what is known as a "shadow" cabinet, and in 1989 Blair was appointed to the position of "shadow" secretary of state for employment. The idea was that if the Conservatives should lose their hold on the government in the next general election, the Labour party would already have its experts in place and be ready to step in.

Labour Party Leader

By 1992, the Labour party had been defeated in four consecutive elections and John Major had succeeded Margaret Thatcher as Prime Minister. Neil Kinnock, the Labour party's leader, resigned in response to this dismal record and his deputy, John Smith, took his place. But then, in May 1994, Smith died unexpectedly of a heart attack. Blair decided he would try for the party leadership position, even though it meant competing against Gordon Brown, an old friend and colleague. Members of the Labour party voted and Blair won, largely because he was regarded as the party's best hope of winning the next general election.

Blair had been working for several years to "modernize" the Labour party, and now he was in a position to really push for change. In the past, the party had strongly supported trade unions, government-controlled industries, and social welfare programs that were paid for by the government. Blair proposed returning industry to private ownership and promoted free enterprise and competitiveness. He took some of the power away from Britain's trade unions, which had traditionally played a major role in choosing candidates and determining the party's policies. He also turned his attention to fighting crime, particularly after the case of Jamie Bulger — a two-year-old who had been murdered by two 10-year-old boys in 1993. This terrible crime had horrified the country and made many people start to worry about Great Britain's rising crime rate. And, finally, he concentrated on raising educational standards and fighting inflation.

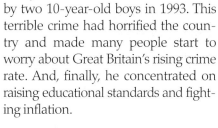

In the 1990s, young people who could not remember a time when the Conservatives had not been in power were drawn to Labour by Blair's energy and youthful appearance. In his speeches he described Labour as no longer a "tax and spend party, but rather a responsible party, a law and order party, a pro-business party."

By the end of Blair's first year as leader, membership in the "New Labour" party had increased by a third. Middle-class voters, who had traditionally seen themselves as Conservatives, began to take notice of the Labour party's new agenda. Young people who could not remember a time when the Conservatives had not been in power were drawn to Labour by Blair's energy and youthful appearance. In his speeches he described Labour as no longer a "tax and spend party, but rather a responsible party, a law and order party, a pro-business party." The British public responded to his message. In the 1997 general election, the Labour party won by a landslide, and Tony Blair replaced John Major as the new Prime Minister.

Prime Minister Blair

In 1997, at the age of only 43, Tony Blair became Britain's youngest Prime Minister since 1812. He moved into 10 Downing Street, the Prime Minister's official London residence, and wasted no time continuing his effort to move the Labour party toward the political center. "The individual thrives best in a well-functioning community of people," he reminded Britons. With that goal in mind, he set out to free the country from its traditional class-consciousness and to minimize racial and economic distinctions.

Blair greeting voters in 1994.

Less than four months after taking office, however, Blair was faced with an unexpected crisis: Diana, Princess of Wales, was tragically killed in a car accident in Paris. He managed to handle the situation with tact and eloquence, referring to Diana as "the people's princess." Diana's death came at a time when she was divorced from her husband, Prince Charles, the future king of England. In the wake of their separation, the royal family had distanced themselves from her. After her death, Blair persuaded the notoriously private royal family that she must be given a public funeral broadcast over loudspeakers so that the British people had an opportunity to participate in the mourning. He also advised the royal family to appear in public at the gates to Buckingham Palace, where flowers and other tributes to Diana were piling up daily. Without putting himself in the spotlight, Blair was responsible for avoiding what could have been a public relations disaster for the royal family and for providing ordinary people with an outlet for their grief over Diana's death.

As Prime Minister, Blair continued the reforms he had begun as head of the Labour party, emphasizing crime prevention and law enforcement, closer relations with the European Union, and improvements in the education and health care systems. He gave Scotland and Wales limited self-government by allowing them to establish regional parliaments of their own. He tackled the issue of British rule in Northern Ireland, which has long been a source of controversy, by opening up communications with

Blair with President Bill Clinton in the Oval Office of the White House, 1996.

Sinn Fein, the political division of the Irish Republican Army. He came out in favor of NATO (the North Atlantic Treaty Organization) taking military action to stop the ethnic strife and bloodshed in Kosovo in 1999; he described the situation there as a "battle of good against evil, between civilization and barbarity, democracy and tyranny." He even went to Moscow to meet with President Vladimir Putin — the first Western leader to do so.

At home, Blair showed that he was serious about changing the face of Great Britain. One of his more controversial moves was an unsuccessful attempt to ban hunting foxes with hounds, a traditional British upper-class sport that also provided jobs for many working-class people. There was a tremendous public outcry, particularly from the upper-class Britons who enjoyed fox hunting and the workers in rural areas who made their living as blacksmiths, gamekeepers, grooms, and other hunting-related occupations. This public outcry caught Blair off guard, and the bill never made it through the House of Lords. An even more radical move was to change the organization of the House of Lords. He abolished the 650 seats for hereditary peers (see box on pages 15 and 16) and replaced them with 500 life peer positions, along with 92 hereditary peers who were allowed to remain until further reforms were passed. His goal was to make the House of Lords less elitist and more "compatible with a democratic society."

Comparisons with President Clinton

At the end of his first year in office, Blair's popularity had actually grown. He had a 72 percent approval rating from the British public — higher than that received by any British Prime Minister at the end of his first year in office since World War II. But after 2000 he began to lose his appeal to voters. Some attributed this to what they called his morally superior attitude and the frequently unpopular stands from which he refused to back down, even when it became obvious that the majority of the British people didn't agree with him. People began to see him less as a fresh-faced idealist and more as a politician. Although he won reelection in the 2001 general election, voter turnout was the lowest it had been in 50 years.

Blair was often compared to Bill Clinton, the American president who was in office throughout most of the 1990s. Blair's youthful good looks and campaigning skills, like Clinton's, had earned him as many votes as his policies; and like Clinton, he was married to a successful attorney with a thriving career. They were also frequently compared due to their political policies. The American press referred to

> *As Prime Minister, Blair wasted no time continuing his effort to move the Labour party toward the political center. "The individual thrives best in a well-functioning community of people," he reminded Britons. With that goal in mind, he set out to free the country from its traditional class-consciousness and to minimize racial and economic distinctions.*

Clinton as a "New Democrat" for his ability to shift the Democratic party's agenda toward the political center. In a similar vein, many said the policies put forth by Blair and his "New Labour" party were moving toward the center and, in fact, were not really all that different from what the Conservative party had supported for years. The British press actually referred to him as "Tony Blinton," or sometimes "Tony Blur," because he had a talent for stating his objectives in broad, non-threatening terms that would appeal equally to middle-class suburban voters and poor and working-class people.

Blair meets with President George W. Bush at the White House, shortly after the terrorist attacks on September 11, 2001.

One thing that set Blair apart from Clinton was his squeaky-clean personal life. Although both he and Clinton had studied at Oxford, Blair had never been caught smoking marijuana or doing anything that might embarrass him in later life. And unlike Clinton, who had a history of extramarital affairs, Blair was obviously devoted to his family and spent as much time with them as he could. Still, his manner, which was often described as "righteous" or "preachy," began to rub voters the wrong way.

Siding with the U.S. in the Iraq War

The United States and Great Britain have had a long history of friendship, which had been cemented by the close personal relationships between Margaret Thatcher and President Ronald Reagan in the 1980s and between Blair and Clinton in the 1990s. Then in September 2001, terrorists attacked the United States, hikjacking airplanes that struck the World Trade Center, the Pentagon, and a field in Pennsylvania. At the World Trade Center, a number of British citizens were also killed. These attacks provoked an outpouring of sympathy and support for America, and the majority of Britons supported the U.S. decision to attack terrorist strongholds in Afghanistan later that year. But then President George W. Bush began to talk about invading Iraq and getting rid of the Iraqi dictator Saddam Hussein. The majority of the British people thought Bush was going too far. Tony Blair, however, steadfastly supported Bush in his plans for war, even when it became clear that the U.S. would go ahead with the invasion without the support of the United Nations. Blair sent British troops to support the U.S. in the Persian Gulf, and his popularity took a sudden nosedive. One of his cabinet ministers even quit in protest.

As the war proceeded and British soldiers began dying, Blair lost much of the support he had gained in the preceding six years. Since most European countries were opposed to the war, Britain's involvement in Iraq undermined attempts to build closer ties between Great Britain and the European Union, an economic and political association of European countries. Then a report by the British Broadcasting Corporation (BBC) said that Blair had "overstated" the facts regarding Iraq's weapons of mass destruction—a primary reason for the invasion. The BBC report said that Blair had done this in order to justify his decision to send British troops to war. The subsequent failure of U.S. troops and weapons experts to uncover any evidence that Iraq was still manufacturing weapons of mass destruction made it look as though Blair had been lying.

Blair steadfastly supported Bush in his plans for war with Iraq, even when it became clear that the U.S. would go ahead with the invasion without the support of the United Nations. Blair sent British troops to the Persian Gulf, and his popularity took a sudden nosedive. One of his cabinet ministers even quit in protest.

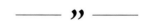

Blair's reputation was soon damaged even further by revelations regarding David Kelly, a weapons expert for the British Defense Ministry who had been named as the source of the BBC report. Kelly committed suicide after being questioned by a parliamentary committee and being overwhelmed by media attention. There was speculation that the government had deliberately subjected Kelly to humiliation, thus contributing to his decision to kill himself. Blair and his government were eventually absolved of blame. A report was issued by a senior judge, Lord Hutton, on how the government had handled the intelligence information it had received prior to the Iraq war. The report declared that, in fact, it was the BBC that was responsible for overstating the case on weapons

Blair addresses British troops on a surprise visit to Iraq. "It's a great honor for me to be here today," he told the troops. "The first thing I want to say is a huge thank you for the work you're doing here."

of mass destruction. Although the head of the BBC stepped down in response to the report, a broad spectrum of the British public still believed that their Prime Minister had involved the country in a war under false pretenses.

British and American casualties in Iraq began to mount, and civil unrest there threatened to undo whatever good the invasion might have achieved. Soon, the strain on Blair began to take its toll. In October 2003 he was hospitalized for several hours with an irregular heartbeat. He returned to his office soon afterward and appeared to be in fine health. But it was clear that his determination to "stay the course" in Iraq—no matter how much it damaged him politically—was making life difficult. Even the capture of Saddam Hussein in December 2003, which Blair hailed as the beginning of "unity, reconciliation, and peace," gave him only a temporary boost in public support.

A Close Call

In January 2004, Tony Blair survived a crisis that could easily have spelled the end of his career as prime minister. Blair is a strong believer in privatization — private funding for industry and public services. He wanted to increase the amount of tuition that British college students paid from about $2,000 a year to $5,400. He insisted that without this additional income, British universities would not be able to compete with those in other countries.

Many Americans are accustomed to paying a high price for their education, so that increase might not sound excessive. But it was an extremely risky position for Blair to take in England, where poor and middle-class families are accustomed to paying very little for their children's education. The issue struck at the heart of what has divided the Labour party ever since Blair took office: "Old Labour" would like to keep the traditional system, under which the government pays for things like higher education and health care, while "New Labour," represented by Blair, wants to require individuals and families to pay more for such services.

When Parliament voted on January 27, 2004, New Labour won, but only by five votes. About 70 members of his own party voted against Blair and the tuition hike — the highest number to do so since the vote supporting Britain's participation in the Iraq war in March 2003. So even though Blair was victorious, the narrow margin of victory was seen as yet another indication of the struggle going on inside the Labour party. Several Members of Parliament claimed that they had been pressured about their votes, which didn't help. As one outspoken MP complained to *The Times,* "All the reasons for voting were to do with dear old Tony — 'Preserve Tony for the nation,''Don't vote with the Tories' — nothing to do with the [tuition] bill."

What Lies Ahead for Blair?

It seems likely that Blair will call for a general election in the fall of 2005. Many critics have charged that he has been spending too much time and energy supporting Bush in Iraq and not enough working on domestic issues like health care, education, and his country's transportation system, and he has recently begun to turn his attention to solving problems at home. But even on controversial domestic issues, like raising university tuition fees, Blair has shown a determination that some people regard as inflexible and unyielding. Once he makes up his mind, he is unlikely to change it — a characteristic that has made some Britons wonder whether he will still be their Prime Minister a year from now. But for the time being, his position appears to be secure.

Blair and his family pose for photographers at their vacation villa in Italy, 2000. Blair, who is holding his new baby, Leo, is accompanied by Kathryn, Euan, Cherie, and Nicky.

MARRIAGE AND FAMILY

In 1980, Blair married Cherie Booth, the young lawyer he had met in Derry Irvine's office when he was just out of law school. Booth uses two forms of her name: she uses her maiden name professionally and her married name when she is acting as the Prime Minister's wife. As one of Britain's most prestigious lawyers, she specializes in employment law. Booth has been named a "Queen's Counsel," which means that she argues legal cases on behalf of her country's government. It's an honor granted to only a small percentage of Britain's lawyers. Although she briefly considered a career in politics herself and actually ran for Parliament as a Labour party candidate in 1983, she has since abandoned politics to work in a human rights law firm and to earn money to support her family. Her work as a lawyer has frequently required her to take stands that oppose those of her husband and his party, but she has managed to keep her career separate from her role as the wife of the Prime Minister. Unlike American First Lady Hillary Clinton, who became a lightening rod for criticism during her husband's presidency, Cherie Booth has avoided negative publicity when she has gotten involved in government policy.

The Blairs live in London and spend their weekends at Chequers, the Prime Minister's country house. They have four children: Euan, born in

1984; Nicholas, born in 1985; Kathryn, born in 1988; and Leo, born in 2000. Cherie Booth made headlines during her husband's first term in office when she announced that she was pregnant at age 45. When Leo, named after Blair's father, was born in May 2000, he became the first child born to a Prime Minister in office in 152 years. Booth insisted that her husband make changes in his work schedule so that he could spend more time caring for Leo, and she has been a role model in many other ways for working mothers.

The Blairs have made a real effort to give their four children as normal an upbringing as possible. Cherie Booth is particularly aware of the dangers involved in having a famous father, since her own father was a well-known television actor; he starred in an English comedy series that was the model for the popular American TV series, "All in the Family." Tony Blair always has breakfast with his children and spends an hour with them at the end of the day, while his wife is often still working. They spend most of their weekends at Chequers and vacation in Europe in the summer.

HOBBIES AND OTHER INTERESTS

On the weekends he spends at Chequers, Tony Blair likes to swim in the pool there. Tennis is his favorite sport, and he can often be seen on the tennis courts at Chequers as well. When his schedule allows, he likes to play football with his children.

HONORS AND AWARDS

Charlemagne Prize (City of Aachen, Germany): 1999

FURTHER READING

Books

Hinman, Bonnie. *Tony Blair,* 2003
Rentoul, John. *Tony Blair: Prime Minister,* 2001
Wilson, Wayne and Jim Whiting. *Tony Blair: A Real-Life Reader Biography,* 2003

Periodicals

Atlantic Monthly, June 1996, p.22; July-Aug. 2003, p.27
Current Biography Yearbook, 1996
New York Times, May 14, 2000, Section 6, p.56
Newsweek International, Sep. 29, 2003, p.24

People, May 19, 1997, p.201
Reader's Digest, Mar. 2003, p.71
Time, Mar. 31, 2003, p.64; June 11, 2001, p.34; Feb. 2, 2004, p.24
Time International, Dec. 10, 2001, p.36
The Times (London), Jan. 28, 2004, p.A3

Online Articles

http://www.theatlantic.com/issues/96jun/blair/blair.htm
   (*Atlantic Monthly,* "The Paradoxical Case of Tony Blair," June 1996)

ADDRESS

Tony Blair
10 Downing Street
London SW1A 2AA
United Kingdom

WORLD WIDE WEB SITES

http://www.number-10.gov.uk/output/page2.asp
http://www.explore.parliament.uk/Parliament.aspx?id=3

Kim Clijsters 1983-

Belgian Professional Tennis Player

BIRTH

Kim Clijsters (pronounced KLEYE-sters) was born on June 8, 1983, in Bilzen, Belgium, a town in the Flemish-speaking region of the country. Her father, Lei Clijsters, was a renowned soccer star, while her mother, Els Vandecaetsbeek, was a champion gymnast. The Clijsters family later resided in the city of Bree, and in 1985 they welcomed another girl, Elke, into the family.

YOUTH

Clijsters grew up surrounded by sports. Her parents were both exceptional athletes, but they never pressured her into a career in sports. Instead, they supported her in all of her pursuits. Clijsters later commented about the physical gifts she received from her parents. "I got my build from my dad. I've never really touched weights or anything. I get my flexibility from my mum. She used to do gymnastics. For a strong girl like me, I think I'm very flexible as well. So I think it's a very good mix to have."

> ――― " ―――
>
> *"I got my build from my dad. I've never really touched weights or anything. I get my flexibility from my mum. She used to do gymnastics. For a strong girl like me, I think I'm very flexible as well. So I think it's a very good mix to have."*
>
> ――― " ―――

Clijsters gravitated towards tennis at the age of five after seeing other children playing the game in a local park. By the age of six, she was already participating in various competitions. A few years later, at the age of eight, she started taking private lessons. Still, her parents were reluctant to push her in that direction. "Tennis is still a hobby to Kim," her father once said. "If one day she doesn't like tennis, she should look for something else to do." Clijsters felt fortunate that her parents had that attitude. "My mum and dad, they've always told me from day one if you don't like it and you don't enjoy anything like traveling, hotel rooms, whatever, that's fine. You don't have to play tennis for us. I'm very lucky," she said.

But Clijsters was determined to succeed in the sport. By 1992, her family asked Bart Van Kerckhove to be her first coach. The move proved to be an important one, and a few years later, Clijsters won the Belgian Junior Championship at the age of 11. Before long, Van Kerckhove and others became convinced that she had the talent to be a world-class tennis player. Clijsters and Van Kerckhove eventually parted ways in 1996.

From there, the rising star went to tennis school in Antwerp. This was another positive experience for Clijsters, as she got a chance to showcase her talents and compete against many top international players her own age. At the training school, Clijsters met tennis coach Carl Maes. The pair hit it off, and Maes agreed to work with her. He once compared her style on the tennis court to her father's style on the soccer field. "Kim is really a very good copy of her father," Maes said. "Physically, she's very strong. Also, mentally, he was a very tough competitor. He wasn't the most elegant, technical player, but he was fun to watch. They are both very intuitive players—they just feel the game."

Soon thereafter, Maes began to accompany her to practices and tournaments all over the world. Her success was immediate, as Clijsters later recalled. "There are so many junior trophies in the attic that I won through the years I don't know what they all are." Her talent soon began to attract attention. By the time she was 15, she received a major break. The Belgian Tennis Federation gave her wild cards into three $10,000 events, giving her the chance to enter the events without actually qualifying. Clijsters did exceptionally well, winning one and making the finals in another. Her performance proved that she had what it took to turn professional.

But things weren't always rosy during this time. "Late in 1998, my mother Els got a very rare liver cancer and was told she only had two months to live," Clijsters once recalled. "I was just starting my career, playing $10,000 tournaments in Belgium, and it was very hard because at home there was always crying in the family. But tennis was good for me because it helped me take my mind off things." Eventually Els Clijsters had a successful liver transplant and made a remarkable recovery.

CAREER HIGHLIGHTS

Going Pro

In 1999, Clijsters entered the professional ranks with a bang. A month before she turned 16, she found herself in the Belgian Open. To the surprise of everyone but Clijsters and her entourage, she advanced all the way to the quarterfinals in the tournament. Later that year, she entered the legendary Wimbledon tournament. Wimbledon is one of many tournaments on the professional circuit of the Women's Tennis Association (WTA). But there are just four tournaments that make up the Grand Slam of tennis: the French Open, the Australian Open, Wimbledon (in England), and the U.S. Open. These are considered the most important tournaments in professional tennis.

Initially, Clijsters was a bit overwhelmed by the idea of playing at Wimbledon. "I have no idea what to expect. All I can do is try to enjoy it," she said at the time. But once again she made a name for herself, upsetting the 12th ranked Amanda Coetzer 6-2 and 6-4 in the third round. (In women's tennis, a player wins a match by defeating her opponent in 2 out of 3 sets, while men must win 3 of 5 sets. The first player to win 6 games usually wins the set, but if their margin of victory is less than 2 games, the set is decided by a tie-breaker. Shorthand notation is often used to show the score of a tennis match. For example, 6-2, 4-6, 7-6 means that the player in question won the first set by a score of 6 games to 2, lost the next set 4 games to 6, and came back to win the match in a third-set tie-breaker.)

Clijsters next had to go up against Steffi Graf, a player whose posters used to adorn her bedroom wall as a youngster. Before the match, Clijsters remarked, "Just going out to play her will be fantastic for me, and I will have to forget all my feelings for what she is and what she has achieved. It's so exciting." Ultimately, the experience proved to be a bit more humbling as her idol and seven-time Wimbledon champ defeated her twice by the score of 2-6. Clijsters was still a bit star-struck months after the match, especially when Graf later announced her retirement from the game. "The honor of being one of the last players to play Steffi is my best memory of 1999. After the match Steffi said to me I played tennis for the future. That meant so much to me."

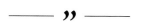

> *"Just going out to play [Steffi Graf] will be fantastic for me, and I will have to forget all my feelings for what she is and what she has achieved. It's so exciting."*

Next up for Clijsters was a spot in the 1999 U.S. Open. In the third round, she faced the hottest star in women's tennis, Serena Williams. Clijsters started strong and almost derailed Williams's eventual championship run. In the third set, Clijsters had a 5-3 lead, but things fell apart when she dropped the last four games. Still, Clijsters viewed the experience as a positive one. "The match against Serena proved that I could play with her and maybe beat her," she remarked. "After that, I felt I wasn't just lucky. I could actually play with the top players."

Clijsters finally won her first WTA title that September at the Seat Open in Luxembourg. Her opponent in the final match was Dominique Van Roost, the No. 1 Belgian player at the time. Clijsters registered identical scores of 6-2 and became the fifth-youngest woman to win a tour event in the 1990s. She finished the year ranked No. 44, a fairly high position for a rookie. Later that year, she also received another honor. A panel of sports writers named her Belgium's Sportswoman of the Year. Soon after, Belgian tennis fans started referring to her as "Our Kim."

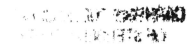

During her rookie season, Clijsters was thrilled to play at Wimbledon against her idol, Steffi Graf, 1999.

Developing Her Game

The year 2000 proved to be another successful one for Clijsters. A tough competitor, she disposed of top players like Anna Kournikova and Arantxa Sanchez-Vicario in various matches. At the U.S. Open she nearly upset Lindsay Davenport. One of her biggest wins came when she beat Elena Likhovtseva to capture the WTA Sparkassen Cup. In all, she played in 17 tournaments in 2000 and finished the year strong, winning 10 of her last 12 matches. She also vaulted 11 places in the player rankings to No. 20 while still maintaining the distinction of being the youngest player in the top 100. This exceptional performance prompted the Belgian sportswriters to name her Sportswoman of the Year for the second consecutive time.

Clijsters continued her upward climb in 2001. In March, she stunned the tennis world by upsetting Martina Hingis at the Tennis Masters Series. The match was a dramatic one, with scores of 6-2, 2-6, and 6-1. Clijsters's performance and dramatic style won over the crowd. In June 2001, she celebrated her 18th birthday by defeating fellow Belgian Justine Henin-Hardenne at the French Open. "I couldn't wish myself a better birthday than this one," Clijsters said at the time. Unfortunately, she later lost in the finals to experienced veteran Jennifer Capriati, but she remained poised and appreciative of all the support she received after the match. "I enjoyed it actually. I felt that I had to give something back to all the Belgian people who came to watch me today." Clijsters also noted the emergence of the other young tennis pros from her home country. "A lot of the new young players try to hit winners on every ball. We try to stay aggressive," she remarked. "If you see all the new upcoming players — Jelena Dokic, Justine Henin, Elena Dementieva — they all hit the ball very hard. I think this is probably the future of tennis." After her performance in Paris, Clijsters rose to No. 7 in the player rankings.

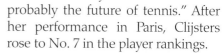

> "People see me differently now, but I feel like the same player I've always been," Clijsters said in 2001.
> "I am really happy with the way my career is going right now. I can't complain. When I was a top-50 player, I used to want to always beat a top-10 player, and now all the top-50 players want to beat me."

The next stop for Clijsters was Wimbledon, and she was ready to put the French Open behind her. "I think Wimbledon is a place where I feel comfortable and I like the grass," she said. "I think I showed at the French Open that I can play at a very high level against the best players in the world. I think I can do well on any surface. Losing in Paris was disappointing, of course, but I take a lot of positives out of it."

This time, Clijsters achieved success at Wimbledon in the women's doubles final. She teamed up with Ai Sugiyama, the top-ranked female doubles player in the world, to defeat Virginia Ruano-Pascual and Paola Suarez by scores of 6-4 in each match. At the time, Ruano-Pascual and Suarez were the reigning French Open doubles champions. Clijsters and Sugiyama then faced the top-ranked Lisa Raymond and Rennae Stubbs in the finals and lost by scores of 6-4 and 6-3. Still, Clijsters enjoyed the experience of pairing up with Sugiyama. "It's my best result ever in women's doubles," she said at the time. "It's nice. We laugh on the court, we make jokes. It's relaxing a little bit." Clijsters didn't fare quite as well in the singles competition, bowing out to Lindsay Davenport by scores of 6-1 and 6-2 in the quarterfinals.

Clijsters rebounded in late July when she competed in the Bank of the West Classic. Suddenly, she wasn't an unknown quantity anymore and people were beginning to take notice of her game. "People see me differ-

Clijsters serves against Justine Henin-Hardenne in the semi-final match of the French Open, 2001.

ently now, but I feel like the same player I've always been," Clijsters re-marked. "I am really happy with the way my career is going right now. I can't complain. When I was a top-50 player, I used to want to always beat a top-10 player, and now all the top-50 players want to beat me." Once again, Clijsters electrified the crowd with her style and flair. In the final match, when she defeated Lindsay Davenport, Clijsters literally burned a hole in her shoe and sock by running up and down the court and skidding her feet against the ground. "I actually bruised my toe. But it's OK, I'm still alive," she said after the match was finished.

But more impressive was Clijsters's game, which netted her $90,000 in winnings and vaulted her to No. 5 in the WTA rankings. "I am really happy to have a title this year," she said. "I've been in the finals, but I never took the extra step to beat the best players. This really means a lot to me." Still, she acknowledged that she still had to improve her game to meet her ulti-mate goals. "I have to keep working. I can still be fitter and serve better.

There are a lot of things I need to work on. I feel like I am getting closer. And I know against the best players, the star players, you just can't make mistakes." Even Davenport admitted that Clijsters had stepped up her game since they met at Wimbledon early in the month. "She is a better player than she was three weeks ago. She didn't play well at Wimbledon. She played will here." Clijsters had continued success through 2001, including a trip to the U.S. Open quarterfinals in September. Ultimately, she lost to Venus Williams 6-3, 6-1 in that tournament.

Continued Success

> "This is definitely my biggest win and it feels incredible," Clijsters remarked after the 2002 WTA Tour Championships. Later, she said that "It's still pretty amazing for me to realize all of this and what I've achieved. I'm only 19. It's incredible."

It wasn't until May 2002 that Clijsters was able to get her revenge against Venus Williams. The stage was the Betty Barclay Cup, and Williams was the top seed and defending champion. Clijsters started the match off horribly, losing 1-6 in the opening set, but she came back strong and finished off Williams 6-3, 6-4.

Clijsters continued her 2002 assault on the Williams family by upsetting top-ranked Serena Williams 7-5, 6-3 at the WTA Tour Championship in November. Clijsters took home the top prize of $765,000 for her effort. "This is definitely my biggest win and it feels incredible," she remarked after the tournament. Later, she reflected further: "It's still pretty amazing for me to realize all of this and what I've achieved. I'm only 19. It's incredible." Williams also had high praise for the Belgian: "She's always done really well and had a lot of talent," she said. "We've always had some pretty competitive matches. She obviously has a very good future. We will see what next year will bring. I think she'll do very well."

At the Australian Open in January 2003, Clijsters once again found herself up against Serena Williams. This time it was Williams's turn to shine. Clijsters won the first set 6-4, but dropped the second 3-6. She was up 5-1 in the third and final set before falling apart and losing to Williams 5-7. Despite the collapse, Clijsters remained upbeat after the match: "I can't blame myself for anything," she said. "I just kept trying to hang in there. It just wasn't good enough at the end. Serena just started playing much more aggressively and hardly made any errors any more. If she plays her best

*Clijsters hugs
Serena Williams
after beating her
7-5, 6-3 at the
WTA Tour
Championships in
November 2002.*

37

tennis, it's very hard to beat her. That's what she did towards the end. Even though I lost, I enjoyed every moment. Big match, center court, and a Grand Slam. I still had a great time out there." Once again, Williams had kind words for her opponent. "Kim's not only a good tennis player, she's a great person, and I think she'll make a great champion because she's always so positive. Even if she's dying, she always looks positive."

Clijsters faced other difficulties in 2003. In a match against Silvia Farina Elia at Wimbledon in July, Clijsters was stung by a bee on her stomach. She still won the match, but the incident did cause some confusion for her on the court. "I didn't know if I should call the trainer or what. And I was very happy I didn't blow up out there, to know that I didn't have any allergies to it. It has never happened to me before and it hurt." Clijsters then advanced to the semi-finals, where she eventually lost to Venus Williams 4-6, 6-3, 6-1.

―――― " ――――

"I can't blame myself for anything," Clijsters said after losing to Serena Williams in the 2003 Australian Open. "I just kept trying to hang in there. It just wasn't good enough at the end. Serena just started playing much more aggressively and hardly made any errors any more. If she plays her best tennis, it's very hard to beat her. That's what she did towards the end. Even though I lost, I enjoyed every moment. Big match, center court, and a Grand Slam. I still had a great time out there."

―――― " ――――

Life at the Top

In August 2003, Serena Williams announced that she would be off the tennis courts for six to eight weeks while recovering from knee surgery. Venus Williams was also banged up and unable to compete. Because of this situation, and because she had a tour-leading six 2003 titles at the time, Clijsters found herself the No. 1 ranked female tennis player in the world. She was the 12th woman to receive the honor since the inception of the rankings in 1975.

While acknowledging her obvious talent and skill, many questioned if Clijsters was worthy of the ranking. They pointed out that she had yet to win a major tournament and stated that the whole situation wouldn't have happened if Serena Williams had stayed healthy. "Kim would probably rather win a Grand Slam than be No. 1," Lindsay Davenport said at the time. "People equate who wins Grand Slams with who is the best player."

Despite such comments, Clijsters took pride in her accomplishment. "This is a very special day I'll never forget. No matter what will happen the rest of my career, no one will ever take that away from me. It's something that I will always have on my resume," she said. "I'm only 20. I don't see the point of starting to worry about Grand Slams," she added.

An Intense Rivalry

In the absence of the Williams sisters, the biggest threat to Clijsters's No. 1 ranking turned out to be fellow Belgian Justine Henin-Hardenne. The pair had known each other since childhood, and Clijsters had fond memories of their relationship. "We grew up together. We've always kept in contact, and it's pretty amazing how we started at the same thing and ended up around the same ranking," she said. Henin-Hardenne also remarked on their closeness: "Kim and me, we are close friends. We speak about everything. But not of tennis. I think it's so good for a little country like Belgium to have two people like us."

"This is a very special day I'll never forget. No matter what will happen the rest of my career, no one will ever take that away from me," Clijsters said after becoming the No. 1 ranked female tennis player in the world. *"It's something that I will always have on my resume. I'm only 20. I don't see the point of starting to worry about Grand Slams."*

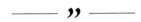

But somewhere along the line, things went sour between Clijsters and Henin-Hardenne. In November 2002, Clijsters decided to skip Henin-Hardenne's wedding to spend time with her boyfriend. In early August 2003, at the Acura Classic in San Diego, Clijsters lost to Henin-Hardenne in the finals. At the end of the first set Henin-Hardenne took an extended time out to get treatment for some blisters on her feet. Clijsters complained that the move was a delay tactic designed to break her rhythm and concentration, something that she said Henin-Hardenne had pulled before with her. "I'm sort of getting used to it, she's done it in every match I've played against her. It didn't look like it was hurting because she was still running." Later she added: "It's a sign that she is not at her best and so she has to resort to other means to get out of scrapes. It is to her credit that she is able to turn matches around by acting this way." Henin-Hardenne, who had previously weathered similar accusations from Serena Williams, disputed Clijsters's comments. "She's disappointed she lost—that's the

Clijsters returns a shot to Henin-Hardenne during the 2003 Acura Classic.

only reason she's saying this," Henin-Hardenne said. "I don't know why all the players are talking about the incidents in my matches because I think I'm a fair player. She said it because she lost the match."

At the time of Clijsters's ascension to No. 1 in 2003, Henin-Hardenne was ranked No. 3. As it would happen, the pair met in the U.S. Open Finals in early September, with Henin-Hardenne once again emerging victorious. She beat Clijsters 7-5, 6-1. The situation turned ugly, this time with Clijsters's father Lei making comments to the press that Henin-Hardenne's gains in muscle and strength over the past year were unnatural and suggesting that the cause was performance-enhancing drugs. "You want me to tell you why Justine is beating Kim regularly?" he asked. "Because her muscle mass has doubled, and she now has an arm like Serena's." These comments enraged Henin-Hardenne and her camp. "I have never been tempted by doping," Henin-Hardenne claimed. "My only doping is my work. I am ready to undergo whatever test, wherever to prove that my body is clean." Carlos Rodriguez, Henin-Hardenne's coach, defended the tennis star and accused Lei Clijsters of jealousy. "In Belgium, what we are trying to do is to start a fight between these two girls. I swear on the heads of my two sons that she has never taken doping products. Justine is better than Kim and will win more often." Later, Clijsters tried to blame the press for the rift between her and Henin-Hardenne. "Everything is the fault of the media," she said. "The Belgian media don't know enough about tennis. They see the gossip that sells papers elsewhere and because we're stars now, they want to create something a little bit like that between us."

Clijsters finished the 2003 season strong, beating Amelie Mauresmo 6-2, 6-0 to win the final tournament of the WTA season, the WTA Tour Championships, with a prize worth over $1 million. "It's a dream come true," she said after the tournament. But when the computer votes were eventually tallied for the whole season, she found herself ranked No. 2, just behind Justine Henin-Hardenne. Still, Clijsters found a silver lining in the rankings. "Of course it's a little disappointing, but at least I got be No. 1. And I end the year No. 2—that not too bad. I made the finals of two Grand Slams," she said.

A Controversial Decision

In December 2003, Clijsters drew heavy criticism from her home country when she announced that she would be skipping the 2004 Olympics in Athens, Greece, because of a conflict with Fila, one of her commercial endorsements. Adidas had the contract to supply the Belgian Olympic athletes with outfits for the games. Clijsters protested because of her existing contract with Fila. The Belgian Olympic committee made a concession and said that Clijsters could wear Fila clothes during tennis matches, but refused to let her wear them in a ceremony if she were to win a medal. International Olympic Committee President Jacques Rogge also criticized the move. "The wearing of the Adidas shirt will show solidarity," he said. "The problem is that 80 percent of athletes don't have enough financial support when they go to the Olympics." Despite such comments, Clijsters remained steadfast in her decision. "As long as my clothing remains an issue, it is impossible for me to go to the Olympics, even though I would like to go and even though I would be able to fit it into my schedule," she explained.

In late January 2004, Clijsters found herself in the finals of the Australian Open. This time her opponent was her nemesis Justine Henin-Hardenne. Although she was nursing a sprained ankle, Clijsters played tough, but eventually lost by scores of 6-3, 4-6, 6-3. As soon as the match ended, Clijsters offered her congratulations by kissing Henin-Hardenne at the net, but later expressed disappointment over the way the match was umpired. Television replays showed that French umpire Sandra de Jenken had

Clijsters stretches for a return during the 2004 Australian Open.

blundered a call that should have had Clijsters making a save on game point. "I'm not the type of player that's gonna start complaining after matches," Clijsters later said. "At the moment it's very disappointing. And a few people have told me that it was in. So that's even more disappointing then. But, you know, I'm not going to blame the umpire or anything because everyone makes mistakes. But of course it's disappointing."

MARRIAGE AND FAMILY

In March 2000, Clijsters was paired with Australian tennis star Lleyton Hewitt in a mixed doubles tournament in Miami, Florida. Later that year, the pair began showing up together at other tennis events, including the French Open and Wimbledon. It was soon confirmed that they were dating and spending as much time together as possible. Clijsters even opted out of a few tournaments so that she could be with Hewitt on the road.

As things heated up between Clijsters and Hewitt, their relationship became a hot topic for the press. "I love being with Kim because she is a great girl," Hewitt declared. "We measure up well. We understand each other and what we have to deal with to be in the top 10 in the world. A different girlfriend probably wouldn't connect." Clijsters also felt that the couple was on the verge of something special. "I know we're both very young, but I feel so comfortable with him," she remarked. "We can't be together every week but that is what makes it special." She continued: "What he does with his career definitely helps me on the court but we hardly talk about tennis. He comes to watch my matches, I watch his, but once we're together, it is different."

On December 23, 2003, Hewitt officially proposed to his girlfriend of four years during a cruise around Sydney Harbor. Clijsters accepted. Later, she commented on how the situation would affect her career: "I don't really plan to have a very long career because one day I wouldn't mind having a family as well. It's hard to put a number on it. It also depends how I'm feeling, the way my body is coping with the tough schedule. See how, you know, if I'm still enjoying it."

Clijsters continues to remain close to her parents and sister, so much so that she decided to build a house in her hometown of Bree on the same street where her parents and grandparents live. Clijsters is thankful for her close relationships with family, and also for the feelings of calm she experiences when she's home with her family in Bree. "It's probably the only place where I can go shopping and go to dinner. Everywhere else, it's different," she said.

"I know we're both very young, but I feel so comfortable with him," Clijsters said about her fiancé, Lleyton Hewitt. *"We can't be together every week but that is what makes it special."* She continued: *"What he does with his career definitely helps me on the court but we hardly talk about tennis. He comes to watch my matches, I watch his, but once we're together, it is different."*

HOBBIES AND OTHER INTERESTS

When she's not playing tennis, Clijsters enjoys spending time with her fiancé and their English bulldog Beauty. She also watches movies like *Gladiator* and *Dumb and Dumber* and cites Madonna, Live, and Savage Garden as her favorite musical acts.

HONORS AND AWARDS

Belgian Sportswoman of the Year (Belgian Sports Journalists Association): 1999, 2000, 2001, 2002
Most Impressive Newcomer (WTA Tour): 1999
Karen Krantzke Sportsmanship Award (WTA Tour): 2000, 2003
WTA Tour Player of the Month (International Tennis Writers Association): November 2002, May 2003, August 2003
Trophy for National Sporting Excellence (Belgian Government): 2002

FURTHER READING

Periodicals

Detroit Free Press, Nov. 22, 2003, p.B2
New York Times, Sep. 4, 2001, p.5
San Francisco Chronicle, July 27, 2001, p.E9
St. Petersburg (Fla.) Times, Aug. 12, 2003, p.C2
Tennis, Mar. 2000, p.16; Mar. 2002, p.44; Feb. 2003, p.79; Apr. 2003, p.12;
    May 2003, p.103
Washington Times, Aug. 18, 2002, p.C11

Online Articles

http://www.dispatch.co.za
    (*DailyDispatch.com*, "Clijsters Has No Complaints," Feb 2, 2004)
http://www.dailytimes.com.pk
    (*DailyTimes.com*, "Beaten Clijsters Opts for Short Career," Feb. 1, 2004)
http://www.theaustralian.news.com.au
    (*TheWeekendAustralian.com*, "Mind Game is Clijsters' Major Hurdle,"
    Jan. 31, 2004)

Online Databases

Biography Resource Center Online, 2004

ADDRESS

Kim Clijsters
WTA Tour
One Progress Plaza
Suite 1500
St. Petersburg, FL 33701

WORLD WIDE WEB SITES

http://www.kimclijsters.be
http://www.wtatour.com/players

Celia Cruz 1924?-2003

Cuban-Born American Singer
Known as "The Queen of Salsa"

BIRTH

Celia Cruz was born in Havana, Cuba, on October 21, some-time between 1924 and 1929. Cruz was always reluctant to reveal the exact year of her birth, but 1924, 1925, and 1929 are the dates most often suggested. Her father, Simon Cruz, was a railroad stoker; her mother, Catalina (Alfonso) Cruz, ran the family household. Her family heritage was Afro-Cuban. Cruz was the second of her parents' four children, but the household also included an extended family of ten other children. Music was an important part of the household, and both her mother and her brother Barbaro enjoyed singing.

YOUTH

Cruz grew up in the Santo Suárez neighborhood of Havana, in what she described as a "poor neighborhood." Living in a big household with an extended family of nieces, nephews, and cousins, Cruz was expected to help out where she could. Because she loved to sing around the house, she was given the task of singing lullabies to younger family members. "I would sit in a chair by their beds and begin singing them to sleep," she recalled. "But, you know, they never went to sleep. And what's more, neighbors would congregate around the door to the house."

> *Because she loved to sing around the house, Cruz was given the task of singing lullabies to younger family members. "I would sit in a chair by their beds and begin singing them to sleep," she recalled. "But, you know, they never went to sleep. And what's more, neighbors would congregate around the door to the house."*

Although Cruz hoped that one day she might sing with an orchestra, like her favorite singer Paulina Alvarez, she didn't seriously think she could make singing a career. Nevertheless, she recalled that "music is what gave me the courage to fight and get out of poverty and touch the universe." As a teenager she began entering—and winning—local talent contests, which fueled her desire to sing.

Cruz's father believed that a musical career wasn't appropriate for a woman, but her mother encouraged her to pursue it. Accompanied by a female cousin, Cruz began accepting jobs around the island. At the time, many radio stations used live performances for much of their programming, so she found jobs singing on the radio. She sang for a week on Radio Progreso Cubana, then had a regular gig on Radio Unión, a station with one of Cuba's most powerful transmitters. This job lasted several months. For these early jobs, Cruz specialized in a type of song called the *pregón*. This was a traditional Cuban song which grew out of the chants and cries that street vendors used to sell their wares.

EDUCATION

Cruz graduated from the República de México school in Havana, and entered the Escuela Normal para Maestros, a school for educators. She planned to teach literature, but dropped out of the Escuela Normal when her singing career took off. She continued her education, however, by studying voice, piano, and music theory at Havana's Conservatory of Music from 1947 to 1950.

FIRST JOBS

While attending the music conservatory, Cruz continued to enter talent contests. In 1947, a local radio station sponsored a talent show

A shot of Cruz from the 1950s, when she was a singer in Cuba with La Sonora Matancera.

called "La Hora de Té." Cruz sang a romantic tango called "Nostalgia," but performed it with the slower tempo of a bolero. She won the contest, and her victory led to several offers to perform locally. "I really loved to sing," she recalled. "But I also did it because if you won, you would get a cake, or a bag with chocolate, condensed milk, ham. We were very poor. All of that came in very handy at home."

Cruz's radio appearances, combined with her musical training, led to even more work. With her family's blessing, she began performing on stage as well as radio, singing with the orchestra Gloria Matancera. She also worked with a female dance troupe, Las Mulatas de Fuego. Her job was to sing along during theatrical numbers and entertain the audience during the dancers' costume changes. This valuable experience, along with her music classes, helped Cruz polish her stage presence and prepare for new opportunities.

CAREER HIGHLIGHTS

Getting Her First Big Break

Cruz got her first big break in 1950, when Cuba's most popular dance band, La Sonora Matancera, lost their lead singer. Myrta Silva had been with the band for over 20 years, but she had decided to return to her native Puerto Rico. Cruz was hired to sing with the band in August 1950 on their weekly radio program for Radio Progreso. Although some fans of Silva complained, Cruz quickly became a valued part of the orchestra. When an American record company executive didn't want her to record with the group, the band's leader offered to repay the recording costs if it didn't sell. The executive had thought no one would want to hear a woman singing a rumba, but the record went on to become a big seller in both Cuba and the United States.

Less than six months after joining La Sonora Matancera, Cruz was regularly making records with the group. That first recording was "Cao Cao Mani Picao/Mata Siguaraya," released in early 1951. Several songs from her first years with the orchestra became standards, including "Yembe Laroco," "Yerbero Moderno," "Caramelo," "Burundanga," and "Me Voy al Pinar del Rio." Cruz and La Sonora Matancera not only performed on radio, but on television and on stage at Havana's famous Tropicana casino. They toured throughout the Western Hemisphere, from the United States and Mexico to Central and South America. They were even featured in five Mexican films, including *Affair in Havana* (1957) and *Amorcito corazón* (1961). Many critics consider Cruz's early years with La Sonora Matancera the "golden era" of her career.

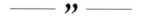

> *Cruz entered talent contests as a teenager, both for the opportunity to perform and for the chance to win prizes. "I really loved to sing,"* she recalled. *"But I also did it because if you won, you would get a cake, or a bag with chocolate, condensed milk, ham. We were very poor. All of that came in very handy at home."*

Leaving Cuba

In 1959, political events in Cuba would lead to a life-changing decision for Cruz. A revolutionary group led by Fidel Castro successfully overthrew the government of Fulgencio Batista. Batista had ruled Cuba as a repressive dictatorship, brutally suppressing opposition to his government. Many people had hoped Castro would create a democratic government, but instead he formed a communist state, allied to the Soviet Union (now Russia). He executed members of the Batista regime and assumed control of the media. Independent newspapers were forbidden, as was any political opposition. Castro's government also took charge of the judiciary and university system. Artistic and intellectual freedoms were severely restricted.

Many Cubans were horrified by the direction of the new government. But it was too dangerous to oppose the government, so some people chose to

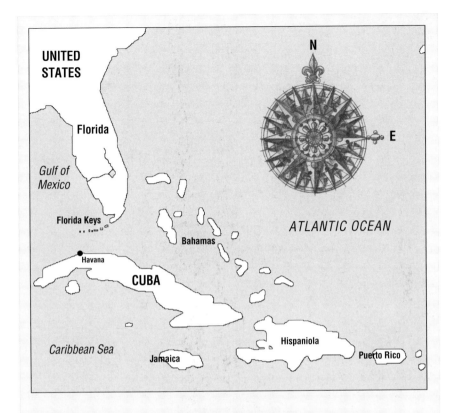

Cuban Music

Cuba in the mid-20th century was a hotbed of popular music, especially dance music. Many popular Latin dance styles grew from Afro-Cuban roots. The rumba was based on a native African dance and grew into a slower, more formal dance called the "sóon." The guaracha was a similar dance with a faster tempo. The mambo, which combined rumba with jazz swing rhythms, was popularized in Cuba in the 1940s. The cha-cha, with its distinctive three-step rhythm (the cha-cha-cha), was a slower kind of mambo. Other Latin dance styles, such as the merengue, tango, and samba, came from other countries in the Caribbean and South America, but were also popular with Cuban audiences. There were differences among the dances in rhythm and tempo (how fast or slow the music was played), but most featured Latin percussion instruments such as the maracas, the claves, the marimbola, and the drums.

leave. Many of these exiles landed in Florida, less than 100 miles north of Cuba. Others wanted to leave, but found their travel restricted by the government. Cruz and the musicians of La Sonora Matancera managed to use one of their tours to escape. Castro's government "wanted us to stay," the singer recalled. "We gave the impression we were just going on another temporary tour abroad." During this tour of Mexico in July 1960, the group announced that they were defecting—in other words, refusing to return to Cuba and renouncing their Cuban citizenship. The Cuban government retaliated by banning their music and refusing them entry to Cuba. Cruz had left her family behind, but she was never allowed into Cuba again, not even to attend her mother's funeral.

> ———— " ————
>
> *Of all the men in the band, it was Pedro Knight who attracted her attention. Not only was he a "gentleman," he honored her talent. As Cruz recalled, he was "the first to approach me and ask if I liked the music, the arrangements, and if the tempo was right for me."*
>
> ———— " ————

Cruz and the orchestra spent a year and a half in Mexico before coming to the United States in 1961. Within a year, she had become an American citizen and was appearing with La Sonora Matancera at Carnegie Hall. In 1962 she also married Pedro Knight, who played first trumpet in the band. While all the men in the band felt protective towards their female singer, it was Knight who attracted her attention. Not only was he a "gentleman," he honored her talent. As she recalled, he was "the first to approach me and ask if I liked the music, the arrangements, and if the tempo was right for me." Knight would later leave the band to become his wife's manager and musical director.

Making Her Mark in America

After moving to America, Cruz cut a deal with Secco Records. She would release more than 20 albums on that label, some with La Sonora Matancera and some without. These albums included *La Incomparable Celia* (1958); *La Reina del Ritmo Cubano* (1959); *La Tierna, Conmovedora, Bamboleadora* (1963); *Sabor y Ritmo de Pueblos* (1965); and her biggest hit for the label, *Canciones Premiadas* (1965). In 1965, after 15 years with La Sonora Matancera, Cruz decided to strike out on her own. She left the orchestra, with Knight as her manager, and also switched labels. On the Tico Records label she would record 13 albums in seven years. Some of these were solo,

La Incomparable Celia *was Cruz's first recording.*

while on several others she performed with the orchestra of Tito Puente, the noted percussionist and bandleader. These albums included *Cuba y Puerto Rico Son* (1966), *El Quimbo Quimbumbia* (1969), and *Algo Especial Para Recordar* (1972).

While Cruz made numerous records during the 1960s and early 1970s, her hard work wasn't rewarded with big sales. Rock 'n' roll was more popular with young Hispanics in America, and her music — traditional songs sung in Spanish — was considered old-fashioned. In addition, she didn't get much promotional support from her record label or from radio stations, so her music didn't reach a wide audience. Cruz sought out that audience herself, however, performing before crowds across the United States and South America. Sometimes she would give as many as six concerts in one day.

Canciones Premiadas *was Cruz's biggest hit for her first label, Secco Records.*

The musical climate took a turn for the better for Cruz in the mid-1970s. Large numbers of Caribbean immigrants came to the United States — immigrants who loved their new country but celebrated their own roots as well. New York City, in particular, had large groups of Afro-Caribbean immigrants from Puerto Rico and Cuba, and Latino culture became widespread. Immigrant musicians began setting traditional Latin dances — sambas, rumbas, cha-chas, and especially the Afro-Cuban guaracha — to a new, modern beat. The result became known as salsa music, a general term that now covers a wide variety of songs that share Latin rhythms. These salsa rhythms soon became very popular. Cruz became part of this new musical wave when she performed in the "Latin opera" *Hommy* at Carnegie Hall in 1973. This musical was a Latin-music version of the classic "rock opera"

Tommy by British rock supergroup The Who. Her part was small but memorable, and it exposed Cruz to a new, younger audience.

Reigning as "The Queen of Salsa"

In 1974, Cruz switched record labels again, signing with the Vaya label on Fania Records. She collaborated with rumba band leader and flutist Johnny Pacheco, who created updated arrangements of many of her La Sonora Matancera classics. Their first album, *Celia and Johnny* (1974), went gold, selling over half a million copies. She recorded two other albums with Pacheco, *Tremendo Cache* (1975) and *Recordando el Ayer* (1976), that continued building her popularity with Latino audiences. Then she branched out to record with the "Fania All-Stars," a group of salsa artists that included other giants of the genre, including Tito Puente, Willie Colon, and Pete "El Conde" Rodriguez. Older audiences loved hearing songs from their youth, while newer fans enjoyed Cruz's creative "scatting" — a fast-paced, improvisational singing style that reminded many critics of jazz great Ella Fitzgerald.

No one knows exactly when Cruz received the label "The Queen of Salsa," but there was no question she deserved it as her career continued. One of the rare female performers in the genre, she was its most visible figure. She sold out concerts in France and Africa in

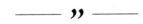

> *Cruz had a stage presence that was both forceful and friendly. Her rich, contralto voice was soulful and powerful, and she was a skilled improviser, able to devise rhymes on the spot. Although her booming voice could fill a room, it could also span octaves, dance quickly from note to note, and sing intricate rhythms. Not only was she a skillful singer, she was a born entertainer.*

the 1970s, including one in 1975 before the famous "Rumble in the Jungle" boxing match between Muhammad Ali and Joe Frazier. She topped "Best Vocalist" polls of the *New York Daily News, Billboard Magazine,* and *Latin N.Y.,* and was awarded keys to the cities of Miami, Dallas, and New York, as well as Union City, New Jersey, and Lima, Peru. In 1982 she recorded a reunion album with La Sonora Matancera, *Feliz Encuentro,* which contained mostly new material. The title track was another chart-topper for Cruz. Whether on stage in front of thousands, or in the studio making records, Cruz was always trying to please her audience.

Cruz had a stage presence that was both forceful and friendly. Her rich, contralto voice was soulful and powerful, and she was a skilled improviser, able to devise rhymes on the spot. Although her booming voice could fill a room, it could also span octaves, dance quickly from note to note, and sing intricate rhythms. Not only was she a skillful singer, she was a born enter-tainer. Wearing glittering, flamboyant costumes, she had a seemingly boundless energy that she shared with her audience. Dancing, joking, waving her arms, and giving her trademark call of "Azucar!" ("Sugar!"), she would leave audiences feeling she had given them everything she had to give—sometimes for as long as three hours. "It is hard to describe the dazzling energy and warmth she was able to convey to an audience," Pulitzer Prize-winning author Oscar Hijuelos wrote in the *New York Times.* "That she could create a rush to the dance floor, and yet do so while maintaining an air of intimacy and connection with her listeners, is a testament to her great personality and charisma as a performer."

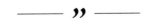

> *"It is hard to describe the dazzling energy and warmth she was able to convey to an audience," Pulitzer Prize-winning author Oscar Hijuelos wrote in the* New York Times. *"That she could create a rush to the dance floor, and yet do so while maintaining an air of intimacy and connection with her listeners, is a testament to her great personality and charisma as a performer."*

A Musical Ambassador

In the 1980s and 1990s Cruz began using her star power to spread salsa to a wider audience. She collaborated with singer David Byrne, of the avant-garde rock group Talking Heads. She also recorded or performed with pop singer Dionne Warwick, soul singer Patti Labelle, opera singer Luciano Pavarotti, and rapper Wyclef Jean, among others. For Cruz, these collaborations weren't marketing gimmicks to appeal to curious listeners—they were just new ways to express her love of music. "We've never had to attract these kids," she said of her younger fans. "They come by themselves. Rock is a strong influence on them, but they still want to know about their roots. The Cuban rhythms are so contagious that they end up making room for both kinds of music in their lives."

It wasn't just young Latinos who made her music part of their lives. Cruz performed to sold out audiences in Japan, Thailand, Morocco, Ireland, Denmark, England, Germany, and all over Latin America. She even en-tered the Guinness Book of World Records in 1987, when she set a record for the largest concert crowd ever. That year some 240,000 fans heard her sing in Tenerife, Spain, at the festival "El Baile del Carnaval."

Cruz appeared in the 1991 film The Mambo Kings *with Antonio Banderas and Armand Assante.*

Cruz also increased her audience through her film and television work. She made appearances in Mexican movies and "telenovelas" (soap operas) in Spanish-language roles. But in 1992 she was given a small part in the film *The Mambo Kings,* an American film about salsa music starring Antonio Banderas and Armand Assante. The director was so impressed by her acting ability that her role was expanded. Cruz understood English but wasn't very confident in her ability to speak it, so it was a great step forward. She followed *Mambo Kings* with an acting turn in another English-language movie, *The Perez Family* (1995), with Marisa Tomei and Angelica Huston.

Cruz had brought salsa music into the mainstream, and she began receiving mainstream recognition. In 1987 she was awarded a star on the Hollywood Walk of Fame. In 1990 she was awarded a special Lifetime Achievement Award from the Smithsonian Institution. She received the prestigious National Medal for the Arts from President Bill Clinton in 1994. Four years later she received a Hispanic Heritage Lifetime Achievement Award, which recognized not only her talent, but also her efforts to raise money for charities ranging from AIDS and cancer research to organizations that aid orphans and handicapped people in Central America. As for musical awards, she received some of the industry's most important honors. In 1989 she won her first Grammy Award, for the Tropical Salsa album *Ritmo en el Corazón*, which she recorded with Ray Barretto. In 1998 she received a Grammy nomination for Best Rap performance by a duo or group for a collaboration with rapper Wyclef Jean. When the Latin Grammy Awards (an international award) made their debut in 2000, Cruz won for her album *Celia Cruz & Friends*. She followed that up with another Latin Grammy the following year for her album *Siempre Viviré*, and a third in 2002 for her smash hit album *La Negra Tiene Tumbao*, which also earned her a second U.S. Grammy Award.

Although she was well past the age of retirement by the year 2000, Cruz showed no signs of slowing down. She sometimes had to trade in her six-inch heels for sneakers because of a knee problem, but she spent most of her time out on the road. When asked if she thought about retiring,

> "
>
> *When asked if she thought about retiring, Cruz said: "Why should I? You would give up your career if you lost your voice for good, or if the impresarios stopped calling, or the audiences stopped coming. But as long as those things are there, I don't plan to stop. There is nothing that makes me feel better than to be with my public."*
>
> "

she said: "Why should I? You would give up your career if you lost your voice for good, or if the impresarios stopped calling, or the audiences stopped coming. But as long as those things are there, I don't plan to stop. There is nothing that makes me feel better than to be with my public." Her public felt the same way, for Cruz always tried to keep her performances fresh. "I always try to shape my repertoire around a particular audience. . . . I'm always changing my outfits, my look onstage."

A Lasting Legacy

Cruz was delighting crowds on television and in concert, from the United States to Latin America to Asia, up until the end of her life. In December 2002, she had surgery to operate on a brain tumor. The surgery did not cure her cancer, and she was in and out of the hospital several times after the operation. She still managed to finish work on her final album, *Regalo del Alma* (2003), although the operation meant she had trouble remembering lyrics. Cruz was at her home in Fort Lee, New Jersey, when she died on July 16, 2003. Tributes came in from all over the world, including from President George W. Bush in the White House. The official newspaper of Cuba's government, which never forgave Cruz for defecting, published only two paragraphs on the death of this legendary performer. But fans in Cuba and all over the world mourned her passing. Memorial services in Miami and New York City drew tens of thousands of grieving fans. Shortly after her death, the city of New York named a music high school in her honor. At the 2003 Latin Grammys, dozens of artists performed a special tribute to this influential trailblazer.

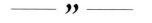

For Cruz, singing was not about the sales or the awards—it was always about the music. "When people hear me sing, I want them to be happy, happy, happy," she once said. "My message is always felicidad—happiness."

Cruz's death renewed the demand for her work. Re-releases of her albums shot to the top of the Latin music charts. At the end of 2003, four Celia Cruz albums were on the Top 10 Tropical Album chart, holding the top three spots. *Billboard* magazine named her their Top Latin Albums Artist of the Year. In addition, her final recording, *Regalo del Alma,* won a 2004 Grammy Award for Best Salsa/Merengue Album. An autobiography based on 500 hours of interviews, *Celia,* was scheduled to appear in July 2004, while actress Whoopi Goldberg hoped to develop and star in a movie based on Cruz's life.

Throughout her lifetime Cruz received a multitude of awards from organizations around the world. She was given several Lifetime Achievement Awards, Hall of Fame citations, and even honorary university degrees, including one from Yale University. She was recognized by the governments of Colombia and the Dominican Republic, as well as the United States. In 1986 the National Ethnic Coalition of Organizations gave her an Ellis Island Medal of Honor. *Billboard* magazine named her to their Latin Hall of Fame in 1994, and the following year gave her a lifetime achievement award. Of the more than 70 albums she recorded, 20 were certified "gold" as selling more than 500,000 copies.

Cruz's final recording, Regalo del Alma, *won a 2004 Grammy Award for Best Salsa/Merengue Album.*

But for Cruz, singing was not about the sales or the awards—it was always about the music. "When people hear me sing, I want them to be happy, happy, happy," she once said. "My message is always *felicidad*—happiness." Her career spanned more than 50 years, and she was known throughout that time as much for her professionalism and kindness as her talent. For Cruz, music was her calling and her gift. As she said upon accepting her Hispanic Heritage lifetime achievement award: "I have fulfilled my father's wish [for me] to be a teacher, as, through my music, I teach generations of people about my culture and the happiness that is found in just living life. As a performer, I want people to feel their hearts sing and their spirits soar."

Cruz performing with her husband, Pedro Knight, in 2002.

MARRIAGE AND FAMILY

Cruz married Pedro Knight, who played first trumpet with La Sonora Matancera, on July 14, 1962. They had dated for two years before their marriage, although they had worked together for 10 years before beginning their courtship. Knight left his career with La Sonora Matancera to become Cruz's manager and musical director. Because of fertility problems the couple never had any children, which Cruz cited as her life's biggest regret. Instead, she spent time with nieces and nephews, and nurtured many young artists as well.

HOBBIES AND OTHER INTERESTS

Although she spent much of her time touring, Cruz thoroughly enjoyed spending time at home with her husband. She enjoyed cooking traditional dishes and spending quiet nights watching television. During her travels she collected recordings of local music, as well as gold coins and gold bracelets. Although Cruz's musical repertoire included sacred songs of the Afro-Caribbean faith known as Santeria, she was a practicing Roman Catholic.

Cruz was involved with several charities, including ones supporting AIDS and cancer research, an orphanage in Honduras, and a fund for the handicapped of Costa Rica. In 2002 she and her husband Pedro Knight established the Celia Cruz Foundation, which helps lower-income students study music and provides aid to cancer patients.

SELECTED RECORDINGS

La Incomparable Celia, 1958
La Reina del Ritmo Cubano, 1959
La Tierna, Conmovedora, Bamboleadora, 1963
Sabor y Ritmo de Pueblos, 1965
Canciones Premiadas, 1965
Cuba y Puerto Rico Son (with Tito Puente), 1966
Quimbo Quimbumbia (with Tito Puente), 1969
Algo Especial Para Recordar (with Tito Puente), 1972
Celia and Johnny (with Johnny Pacheco), 1974
Tremendo Cache (with Johnny Pacheco), 1975
Recordando el Ayer (with Johnny Pacheco), 1976
Celia Cruz and Willie Colon, 1977
Brillante, 1978
Feliz Encuentro (with La Sonora Matancera), 1982
The Winners (with Willie Colon), 1987
Ritmo en el Corazón (with Ray Barretto), 1988
The Best of Celia Cruz, 1992
Irrepetible, 1996
La Vida es un Carnival, 1998
Celia Cruz & Friends: A Night of Salsa Live, 2000
Siempre Viviré, 2000
La Negra Tiene Tumbao, 2001
Regalo del Alma, 2003

HONORS AND AWARDS

Ellis Island Medal of Honor (National Ethnic Coalition of Organizations): 1986
Awarded a Star on the Hollywood Walk of Fame: 1987
Grammy Awards: 1989, Best Tropical Latin Performance, for "Ritmo en el Corazón"(with Ray Barretto); 2002, Best Salsa Album, for *La Negra Tiene Tumbao*; 2004, Best Salsa/Merengue Album, for *Regalo del Alma*
Lifetime Achievement Award (Smithsonian Institution): 1990
Presidential Medal (Government of Colombia): 1990
National Medal of the Arts (National Endowment for the Arts): 1994
Named to Latin Hall of Fame (*Billboard* Magazine Awards): 1994
Casandra Award for International Artist of the Year (Dominican Republic): 1995, 1996

Lifetime Achievement Award (*Billboard* Magazine): 1995
ACE Award for "Extraordinary Figure of the Year" (Association of
   Entertainment Critics): 1996
Hispanic Heritage Lifetime Achievement Award (Hispanic Heritage
   Foundation): 1998
Latin Grammy Awards: 2000, Best Tropical Salsa Performance, for *Celia
   Cruz and Friends: A Night of Salsa;* 2001, Best Traditional Tropical Album,
   for *Siempre Viviré;* 2002, Best Salsa Album, for *La Negra Tiene Tumbao*

FURTHER READING

Books

Contemporary Hispanic Biography, Vol. 1, 2002
Contemporary Musicians, Vol. 22, 1998
Dictionary of Hispanic Biography, 1996
Latino Americans, 1999
Notable Hispanic American Women, Book 1, 1993

Periodicals

Billboard, Oct. 28, 2000, p.50
Current Biography Yearbook, 1983
Hispanic, Nov. 2002, p.54
Latin New York, Oct. 1982 (special Cruz issue)
Los Angeles Times, July 18, 2003, sec.5, p.8
Miami Herald, July 17, 2003, p.A1; July 20, 2003, p.M7
New York Times, Nov. 19, 1985, p. C17; Aug. 30, 1987, sec.2 p.14; July 23,
   2003, p.A19
People, Aug. 4, 2003, p.69
Time, July 11, 1988, p.50
USA Today, July 17, 2003, p.D1

Online Databases

Biography Resource Center Online, 2004, articles from *Contemporary Hispanic
Biography,* 2002; *Contemporary Musicians,* 1998; *Dictionary of Hispanic
Biography,* 1996; and *Notable Hispanic American Women,* 1993

WORLD WIDE WEB SITE

http://www.celiacruzonline.com

THE DONNAS

Brett Anderson (Donna A.) 1979-
Torry Castellano (Donna C.) 1979-
Maya Ford (Donna F.) 1979-
Allison Robertson (Donna R.) 1979-

American Rock Group

EARLY YEARS

The hard rock, all-female group known as The Donnas includes four young women who have been friends since elementary school: vocalist Brett Anderson (Donna A.), born on May 30, 1979; drummer Torry Castellano (Donna C.), born on

January 8, 1979; bassist Maya Ford (Donna F.), born on January 8, 1979; and guitarist Allison Robertson (Donna R.), born on August 26, 1979. (Castellano and Ford share the same birthday by coincidence; they are not twins.)

———— " ————

"Maya and I were playing bass and guitar together early on," says Robertson. "We thought about having a band, but we really didn't have any friends to round one out. It was impossible finding people that knew how to play. Then we thought of the idea of asking people to learn how to play drums and sing so we could eventually form a band. It wasn't a plan to control the world and be big superstars. It was started as kind of a joke on the other bands in our school — which, in our town, were all formed by these popular, blond rich guys trying to be like Nirvana."

———— " ————

Little has been reported about the individual members' childhoods or parents. Allison Robertson is the only one whose parents had experience in the music business — her father, Baxter, is a guitarist, songwriter, and session recording artist. All four girls grew up in Palo Alto, California, near San Francisco, otherwise known as the Bay Area.

FORMING THE BAND

The girls all attended school in Palo Alto, where they all knew one another and were friends. By the eighth grade at Jordan Middle School, Robertson (guitar) and Ford (bass) already had an interest in playing rock music. "Maya and I were playing bass and guitar together early on," says Robertson. "We thought about having a band, but we really didn't have any friends to round one out. It was impossible finding people that knew how to play. Then we thought of the idea of asking people to learn how to play drums and sing so we could eventually form a band. It wasn't a plan to control the world and be big superstars. It was started as kind of a joke on the other bands in our school — which, in our town, were all formed by these popular, blond rich guys trying to be like Nirvana." The middle school had a lunchtime performance opportunity at which many of the school's "boy bands" would play. "The cool thing was to be in bands," said Ford, "so they were all going to play. And there weren't any girl bands playing so we decided to play the show."

From left: Donna F. (Ford), Donna C. (Castellano), Donna R. (Robertson), and Donna A. (Anderson).

Robertson and Ford had heard Anderson singing in the hallways and asked her to be part of the band, and they also asked their friend Torry Castellano if she'd be interested in learning to play the drums. "I had never played drums before," said Castellano. "And Donna R. and Donna F. had only been playing guitar and bass for two months or something. And Donna A. had never sung before in front of people. So a month before the show, we were just like, 'All right let's just do it.' So we practiced and practiced and practiced." Castellano rented a drum kit and learned to play. But it was set up backwards, which she only found out after some of the boys made fun of her.

Screen

The band's first public appearance was at Jordan Middle School's "Day on the Green" on June 8, 1993. They played four "cover" tunes (songs written and performed by others) by The Muffs, Shonen Knife, and Syndicate of Sound. "We didn't have time to learn how to play *and* write songs, you know?" said Castellano.

"We didn't want people to make fun of us because they already made fun of us," guitarist Robertson remembers. "Obviously, news would travel fast that these geeks were gonna form an all-girl band. So in trying to come up with a name, we, like, searched the dictionary for something you couldn't make fun of." They settled on "Screen," a name that wouldn't necessarily mean anything—or provide a reason for anyone to tease them. Other bands appeared under the names "Invisible Purple Butterflies" and "Verbal Constipation."

> ———— **"** ————
>
> *"We didn't want people to make fun of us because they already made fun of us," Robertson remembers. "Obviously, news would travel fast that these geeks were gonna form an all-girl band. So in trying to come up with a name, we, like, searched the dictionary for something you couldn't make fun of." They settled on "Screen," a name that wouldn't necessarily mean anything.*
>
> ———— **"** ————

Reaction from their fellow students was not positive. Despite the comical names of the other bands appearing, the audience found ways to make fun of the newly formed Screen: "Screen? I oughta screen your calls," or "You should be Screen and not heard," and "Screen? What a stupid name! How about the Hockey Pucks?" "From then on, we were lepers," recalls Ford. "Everyone thought we were big weirdos — Satan worshipers, drug addicts, lesbians." Anderson remembers, "It was like, 'Okay, you're never, ever going to be popular.'But it wasn't that much of a gamble. We already didn't have friends."

Ragady Anne

The girls spent the following summer practicing hard in the Castellano garage and writing their own songs, in addition to learning more cover tunes. The first song they wrote was "Tammy the New Feminist," which made fun of the type of girl they thought many of their peers thought they were.

When they entered Palo Alto High School in the fall of 1993, they'd changed the band's name to Ragady Anne. Despite the name change, the teasing only seemed to get worse. "We'd be walking to class and the singer in this band called Smiley Face—he was popular and had a really big ego—would follow us around going, 'Ragady Anne! I love Ragady Anne! I looooove them! They're so awesome," says Robertson. "He'd be screaming it behind us."

The reaction of others only served to motivate the young musicians. "We dealt with so many people hating us that it really brought us together," remembers bassist Ford. "If one of us had gotten sick of being in the band, there wasn't really anything else to do or anybody else to be friends with." They kept practicing, writing songs, and performing whenever they had the chance. Their second public performance was as Ragady Anne on November 6, 1993, at a "battle of the bands," at which, according to the band's web site, they "blew everybody off the stage." They also participated as Ragady Anne in a Christmas Benefit, a food and toy drive for disadvantaged families in the Bay Area (the band continues to participate every year). They released a 7" vinyl record with independent recording label Radio Trash, which included a single called "Freakshow" about breakfast cereal.

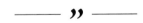

"From then on, we were lepers," recalls Ford. "Everyone thought we were big weirdoes — Satan worshipers, drug addicts, lesbians." Anderson remembers, "It was like, 'Okay, you're never, ever going to be popular.' But it wasn't that much of a gamble. We already didn't have friends."

During this time the members of the band began listening to and performing the music of harder rock bands that were popular in the late 1970s and 1980s, including Kiss, AC/DC, Metallica, and Motley Crue. To reflect this new edge in their repertoire (and because there were already other bands named "Ragady Anne"), the girls chose a new name: "The Electrocutes."

The Electrocutes and The Donnas

As the band's musical style began to solidify, others began to notice them. They caught the attention of Bay Area promoter Mark Weiss, who gave the band one of their earliest professional gigs. "They weren't faking anything; they were just being themselves," Weiss said. "They were unconscious of how good they were." Singer Anderson describes the music of The Electrocutes as "speed metal." She said, "The Electrocutes were kind of confusing and enigmatic; we understood it but nobody else did."

Soon, another opportunity emerged with Darin Rafaelli, a local musician, songwriter, promoter, and owner of a small independent label. He heard the girls play live and asked them if they'd like to be part of a project he'd conceived for his Super**Teem record label. "He was like, 'Yeah, you guys are great. I've been looking for a girl band. Do you guys want to play some

Their first CD, The Donnas, *was released on an independent label.*

rock songs, rock 'n' roll?' We were like, 'OK, whatever, that sounds cool.'" Rafaelli had written some songs for an all-girl band and needed a group to perform them. The music was less edgy than the hard-driving music the Electrocutes had been performing, and the band's name didn't quite fit what has been described as the "bubble gum punk" music written by Rafaelli.

The name "The Donnas" came about when the band manager was doodling on a McDonald's "Happy Meal" box. But the name was also a nod to the influence of a 1970s and 1980s punk rock band, The Ramones. The members of the Ramones (Joey, Dee Dee, Johnny, and Marky) all claimed to share the same last name. Instead of having the same last name, however, The Donnas would each have the same first name, using the first letter of their actual last names to differentiate them. It was a gimmick, and calling the Rafaelli project The Donnas enabled the band to continue playing and writing as The Electrocutes.

"We always thought of The Electrocutes as our artistic outlet, our baby, you know. And then The Donnas was just a side project," said Anderson. While the girls wrote and recorded with Rafaelli as The Donnas, they continued playing live as The Electrocutes. "It was kind of fun, because we really took The Electrocutes seriously, but with the Donnas, we could just eat tacos and write a song in a few minutes and that was it," says drummer Castellano.

Their First Release: *The Donnas*

The Donnas released three singles and one album with Rafaelli's Super** Teem label. Their first album, called *The Donnas*, was recorded in a single day and released in January 1997. "It was always a joke for us," said guitarist Robertson. "Not a bad joke, but, like a fun joke—this fake band that was from South City and wore matching outfits. It was kind of silly. We didn't think people would really buy into it."

> "
> *"It was kind of fun, because we really took The Electrocutes seriously, but with the Donnas, we could just eat tacos and write a song in a few minutes and that was it,"says drummer Castellano.*
> "

The group's dual public images soon offered some interesting ironies. The Electrocutes were a hard-driving speed metal act and The Donnas were a pop-punk outfit. As The Electrocutes, they would publicly slander The Donnas as a "goody goody" band. Among other things, The Donnas would wear matching T-shirts with the band's name on it, which the girls considered part of the joke. Once, they even performed live on a radio show, as the two different bands. "Because you couldn't see us, it was a good little joke."

But The Donnas were catching on faster than The Electrocutes—even as far away as Japan. In the spring of 1997, during the girls' senior year at Palo Alto High School, they got their first taste of rock and roll stardom. The owner of a record store in Tokyo invited them to come and play and offered to pay for it. "This guy owned a tiny little record store in Tokyo—I'm talking the size of someone's bathroom—crammed with records," remembers Robertson. "He carried our albums and they were selling like hotcakes. . . . We stayed in his friend's house and slept on the floor, freezing. But once we got to the shows, they were all jam-packed. That was the first time we ever saw a group of people singing our lyrics."

American Teenage Rock 'n' Roll Machine

When it became time to think about recording a second album, the band members agreed they wanted to exert more creative control and to rely less upon the direction of Rafaelli. Some have compared the influence of the older Rafaelli (in his mid-30s) to that of a "Svengali," essentially a puppet-master who controlled them from behind the scenes. Others have compared him to famed rock and roll producer Phil Spector (The Kinks, The Ramones, and many others), who controlled every detail of a band's sound. But band members describe the relationship differently. "We were writing songs before we ever met Darin, so it's not like we started playing and someone else was writing our songs," says Anderson. "Then we met him and started making this kind of music and after awhile, no one was taking us seriously because they saw him and immediately went, oh, they're not really friends, he's telling them what to do, he's the Svengali/ Phil Spector to their puppets — as if there wasn't a possibility for anything else to happen!"

> "I thought they were so cool," said Lookout co-owner Molly Neuman. "It was extremely charming to see these 17-year-old girls singing these funny, catchy, one-and-a-half minute songs."

For their next album, *American Teenage Rock 'n' Roll Machine*, the girls decided not to rely solely on Rafaelli for all the material. Instead, they contributed four songs they originally wrote without Rafaelli for The Electrocutes. Among these songs were "Looking for Blood," "You Make Me Hot," and "Speed Demon." As Anderson says, "We finally just merged them together, so instead of saving all of our ideas for the Electrocutes, we used them for the Donnas." But they also continued occasionally co-writing with Rafaelli and performing his songs.

In the summer of 1997, the year the girls graduated from high school, they were approached by the independent punk rock label Lookout — whose signed bands included Green Day and Rancid. The girls had not entirely given up on The Electrocutes as a concept, but the label was more interested in The Donnas. "The Donnas had a bigger profile," said Lookout co-owner Molly Neuman. "I thought they were so cool. It was extremely charming to see these 17-year-old girls singing these funny, catchy, one-and-a-half minute songs."

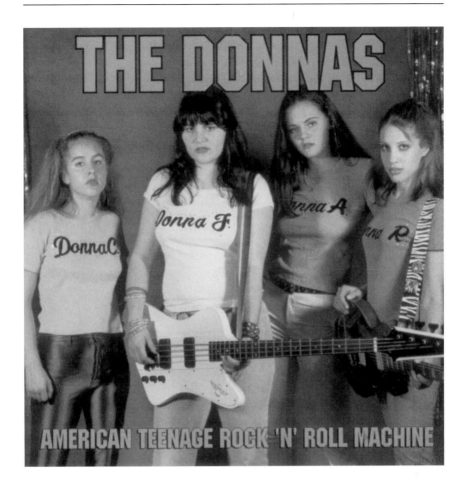

Lookout signed the band to a recording contract and produced their second album, *American Teenage Rock 'n' Roll Machine*. According to guitarist Robertson, "The first album sounds garagey and was recorded in one day. *Rock and Roll Machine* was recorded in two days. In a studio." The new album, released in 1998, received favorable press, and the band was offered the opportunity to go on tour. But by then the girls, recently graduated from high school, had all headed off for college.

EDUCATION

Even while the band was in their intensely active formative phase, they made their school work a priority. "Our high school was a really good high school—everyone did well," says bassist Ford. "We're all smart, and it wasn't hard to do really well. Also, if you do well in school then your parents worry about you less, you can stay out later. They trusted us more." All four young women graduated from Palo Alto High School in 1997.

That fall, despite the success of the band so far, all four started college. Ford and Robertson went to the University of California at Santa Cruz, Anderson to the University of California at Berkeley, and Castellano went to New York University. But they had just signed a contract with a label that had done well for other bands, and the college experiment did not last long. They dropped out of school, and The Donnas were soon reunited. "It was like, 'yeah, I'd much rather hang out with these people rather than all these stupid new people in college,'" recalls Robertson.

CAREER HIGHLIGHTS

Breaking Away

The collective decision of Anderson, Castellano, Ford, and Robertson to leave college was a turning point in their pursuit of a career in the music business. As they got down to touring and writing and practicing, the group decided to break from Rafaelli and go it alone. "We didn't want to be stuck in some band where some dude wrote the songs for us," said guitarist Robertson.

Other members of the band describe the parting in more diplomatic terms. "People didn't really understand that it was just, like, five friends writing songs together and stuff," says drummer Castellano. "They kind of had this idea of this older guy/younger girl thing where he had all the control, which is not true at all. And I think he was kind of tired of people perceiving it that way and so were we. You know, we'd been a band for, like, three years before we even met him, so we wrote a lot of songs before we even met, and we kind of wanted to just go back to writing by ourselves."

Singer Anderson credits Rafaelli with helping them to write songs that would sell. "I think his biggest contribution is that he taught us, like, how to keep songs simple enough for people to latch onto them," she said. "We were into our [instrumental] abilities so much that the songs were inaccessible."

Get Skintight

In 1998, The Donnas toured extensively by van and bus to support their first two albums. At the same time, they wrote and perfected the sound they wanted for the third album, which was to be called *Get Skintight*. For this album, they decided to spend a little more time in the studio and used

producers Jeff and Steve McDonald, who'd produced the Los Angeles-based punk group Red Kross. The McDonald brothers had seen The Donnas perform live and talked their way into letting them produce the upcoming CD.

"This time," says Castellano, "We had 10 days, so we did a lot of different takes, even if we did it perfect the first time." *Get Skintight* was released in 1999 and included rocking songs like "Get Out of My Room," "Hot Boxin'," "Doin' Donuts," and a cover of metal band Motley Crue's "Too Fast For Love."

Other highlights of the band's early days as full-time professionals were opening for the glam-metal rockers Cinderella in Las Vegas and veteran rocker Joan Jett in New York City. They also appeared in two teen films,

Jawbreaker and *Drive Me Crazy*. For *Drive Me Crazy*, the band had to play a cover of REO Speedwagon's "Keep On Lovin'You," a ballad they detested. The film's producers wanted The Donnas to play something softer than their usual fare. "We got tricked into doing it," said Ford. "We wanted to do Bon Jovi or Guns 'n' Roses, and then they just made us play that. We were, like, 'We'll do anything else!'" They also covered the Kiss 1970s hit "Strutter" for the film *Detroit Rock City*, which was produced by Kiss bassist Gene Simmons.

The Donnas Turn 21

By this point, the band members were growing up. The first three albums were largely about being high school girls. But their fourth album, *The Donnas Turn 21*, released in 2001, was about becoming young women, with a lot of humor woven in. "We just write about having fun," Anderson said in an interview at that time. "We'll be doing that until we're 31. We have more to write about now, we travel a lot, we meet more guys, y'know? I think touring is a lot more eventful than high school."

Many of the songs reflected the band's growing emotional and sexual maturation. Despite the suggestiveness of some of the lyrics, there is none of the blatant lewdness that can be found in much of today's popular music. And music reviewers praised the band's improved musical ability and their more polished sound. "Our sound's changed a lot," said Anderson at the time of the CD's release. "We used to sound like a really garage band, it's just that the recordings early on were so terrible. Production-wise the new album sounded so much better than *Get Skintight*."

The Donnas were enjoying a certain amount of notice from regional fans and critics, but they hadn't yet received national attention. Their manager, Molly Neuman, who was also co-owner of the independent label Lookout, began helping the band make the next big step. Drummer Castellano put it this way: "There's only so far you can go on an independent label. It would have been nice to be on Lookout forever, but there's no way that you're going to get very far on the radio with an independent label."

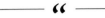

> The Donnas Turn 21 *was about becoming young women, with a lot of humor woven in.* "We just write about having fun," Anderson said. "We'll be doing that until we're 31. We have more to write about now, we travel a lot, we meet more guys, y'know? I think touring is a lot more eventful than high school."

Hitting the Big Time: *Spend the Night*

For their fifth album, the band and manager Neuman agreed that it was time to sign to a major label. Atlantic Records saw the band's potential and had much more to offer in terms of promotional support and distribution than the independent Lookout label. There was some fear, though, among band members that they might lose some of what they enjoyed at Lookout—an attentive staff, complete artistic control, and enthusiasm for everything the band did.

"It's a nurturing feeling when the people putting out your album are really excited about it," said Robertson, about the transition from an "indie" label to a corporate giant like Atlantic. "It's kind of nice to feel that here as well. The stress came with the recording. There were a lot of different opinions on how it should be recorded, where it should be recorded, who should produce it. We thought we were going to be able to do it the way we always do it. Then we kind of panicked, we were afraid the songs wouldn't come out the way we had written them," she said. They were able to bring in the producer they wanted, Robert Shimp, and together with him they worked on demos (practice recordings) of all the songs before actually recording the album. Gradually the band began to appreciate the benefits of additional input from other recording professionals brought in by Atlantic. "You don't need someone telling you what to do, but you do need more checks and balances," said Robertson.

——— " ———

"Nobody ever forces anything on us," Robertson says, "but occasionally someone will say something to the effect of 'Maybe it could use a little extra guitar here,' or 'What about these vocals? Maybe you should add some harmonies'— stuff like that. But we're a band with one guitar and one vocalist, and we have to be conscious of that. . . . We're always asking ourselves, 'Will it hold up onstage?'"

——— " ———

On one point, though, The Donnas stood their ground. The Donnas strongly opposed using high technology studio techniques that would have resulted in what they felt was not their true sound. Guitarist Robertson is adamant about not doing anything in the studio that can't be reproduced onstage. "Nobody ever forces anything on us," she says, "but occasionally someone will say something to the effect of 'Maybe it could use a little extra guitar here,' or 'What about these vocals? Maybe you should add some harmonies'— stuff like that. But we're a band with one guitar and one vocalist, and we have to be conscious of that, or we'll end up with this big slick project that we then have to take out on the road. . . . We're always asking ourselves, 'Will it hold up onstage?'" Singer Anderson agrees: "Touring, you learn a lot about your instrument, what you can and can't do. We're very strict about only writing things that we can pull off really tight live. We don't want anything to sound better on the album than it does on stage."

The Donnas pose in downtown San Francisco. From left: Donna R. (Robertson), Donna A. (Anderson), Donna C. (Castellano), and Donna F. (Ford).

The band's sense of their own identity as a group, coupled with Atlantic's production and promotional savvy, has spelled success for The Donnas so far. Their transition to a major national label brought them this kind of review from *Rolling Stone* reviewer Michael Ansaldo:

> From the first seconds of *Spend the Night's* feral opener, "It's on the Rocks," it's clear that the major-label jump has done nothing to soften the group's edges. Tracks like "Take it Off," "Too Bad About Your Girl," and "Take Me to the Back Seat" rock with the same exaggerated badness as their first four albums. If anything the big-budget production fully reveals the rock chops that previous releases only hinted at, and *Spend the Night* boasts a sonic punch that places it confidently between AC/DC's *Powerage* and Judas Priest's *British Steel* on your CD shelf.

Suddenly the band was enjoying a lot of success. Their new album began getting positive reviews, their songs "Take it Off" and "Who Invited You" began getting radio air play, and the band began getting invitations to appear as musical guests on the "Tonight Show with Jay Leno" and "Saturday Night Live." Their video production of "Take it Off" was in rotation on MTV, and they appeared in a Budweiser commercial.

In early 2003, the band launched a tour as the headliner, no longer as the opening band. "We have so many things planned," said drummer Castellano, "and so many things are happening that we have to concentrate on what's happening right now. I think you have to kind of look at the big picture, but also it can get a little overwhelming, so you have to look at what's right in front of you. I think you have to just keep on going."

> *"We know each other better than we know ourselves," Anderson said. "We know when to leave each other alone and when we need each other. When we're on the bus and one of us seems irritable, that's when we give her space. We try not to press each other. It's just common courtesy. We try to respect each other."*

Their recent stardom has been hard won, with ten years of ups and downs holding The Donnas together. "We know each other better than we know ourselves," Anderson said. "We know when to leave each other alone and when we need each other. When we're on the bus and one of us seems irritable, that's when we give her space. We try not to press each other. It's just common courtesy. We try to respect each other." Anderson says the respect comes from "knowing that everyone in the band is important, irreplaceable. When you realize that, respect is easy. And you know what? We like each other too."

The Image of the Band

With the popularity the band has earned in recent years has come the challenge of dealing with their public image and how that matches their real lives. "I feel sometimes we have people fooled, because part of The Donnas is that it's larger than life and it has nothing to do with what we're like in person," Robertson says. "I think people would be sad to find out that when I'm not on tour I hang out at my house—I'm a total homebody." Castellano comments about the hard-work side of being in the band: "Sometimes people think that we are just wild and crazy, that we never have to be responsible, we never have to take anything seriously and this isn't a job. So, that's hard to hear too, because we do put a lot of hard work

into it. We try hard to play the best we can every night, and we do have to do lots of interviews and meetings and crazy business stuff."

In terms of their physical appearance, The Donnas prefer a straight-ahead approach that is consistent with their approach to rock music. "We don't get the free clothes or borrow stuff because we don't have a stylist," Robertson says. In fact, during one photo shoot for a magazine the publication's stylist insisted she wear what she calls "a turquoise fur pimp coat, something that Kid Rock or Poison's Bret Michaels or Ludacris would wear—but not me. It's my life and my body." She dug her heels in and refused to wear the outfit: "You either have to go with the flow and be bummed later when you see the picture . . . or stand your ground and people might end up saying you're hard to work with."

Publicly, at least, The Donnas prefer the grungy, garage band look, including T-shirts, jeans, and messy hair. "I wash my hair like four times a month

—— " ——

Reflecting on the band's recent status as a rock and roll force on the national scene, Ford makes a statement that recalls their early days at Jordan Middle School in Palo Alto: "I feel like we don't fit in. I don't think we want to be women in rock. We just want to be rock."

—— " ——

but not necessarily once a week," says Robertson. Bassist Ford echoes the sentiment, saying, "I like having my hair in my face when I rock out. I can't have a ponytail." Of the band's image, Ford says, "I don't think we're that made up. In every picture, we're in jeans, but we don't have a really polished, made-up image at all."

Reflecting on the band's recent status as a rock and roll force on the national scene, Ford makes a statement that recalls their early days at Jordan Middle School in Palo Alto: "I feel like we don't fit in. I don't think we want to be women in rock. We just want to be rock."

MAJOR INFLUENCES

The first major influences on The Donnas were bands that were receiving a lot of radio play while the band was first forming, like R.E.M. and XTC. Guitarist Robertson says, "If you can imagine the biggest, weirdest R.E.M. fans, that was me and Maya [Ford, bassist] before we formed our band."

When they entered high school, however, they began listening to and playing covers of earlier rock and roll music, including The Ramones, and especially metal bands like Alice Cooper, Kiss, Cinderella, AC/DC, Cheap Trick, and Motley Crue. The Donnas also mention the influence of prominent female-fronted bands of the same era, including Chrissie Hynde and The Pretenders and Deborah Harry and Blondie.

MARRIAGE AND FAMILY

Only one of The Donnas, Allison Robertson, is married. Her husband is Robert Shimp, who produced *Spend the Night*. The other members date and often have steady boyfriends. None of the band members have any children, though.

"You know, when we really like a boy, we get really excited," says drummer Castellano. "We all have different kinds of guys that we like. We may all think one guy is really cute and agree on it and everything, but we don't ever compete."

Their social lives revolve around one another and their families, who remain the band's biggest fans. "We'll be getting ready to go out to dinner," says Ford, "and my parents will be wearing Donnas T-shirts and I have to ask them to change. They're super excited about it."

HOBBIES AND OTHER INTERESTS

It would be safe to say that the common interest all four women share is a love for rock and roll. But they still have other interests as well. For example, in May 2003, The Donnas celebrated their tenth anniversary together as a band. They were on tour in Japan at the time. They took the opportunity to celebrate their big day together at Tokyo Disney. "I know, I know, I know," laughed Robertson, "We're total cornballs. We're the kind of people who would go there anyway, but going there on a big occasion, that's our style."

The band's official web site lists some of the group's individual interests. Brett Anderson, vocalist, enjoys making lasagna. Torry Castellano, drummer, likes "playing drums, hanging out, watching movies, and shopping." Donna Ford, bassist, claims her hobby is drawing pictures of Richard Nixon. And guitarist Allison Robertson enjoys collecting toys and shopping.

RECORDINGS

The Donnas, 1998
American Teenage Rock 'n' Roll Machine, 1998
Get Skintight, 1999
The Donnas Turn 21, 2001
Spend the Night, 2002

FURTHER READING

Books

Contemporary Musicians, Vol. 33, 2002

Periodicals

Boston Herald, Feb.7, 2003, p.S25
Denver Post, Feb. 21 2003, p.FF3
New York Post, Feb. 7, 2003, p.58
New York Times, Nov. 24, p.L4
New Yorker, Apr. 2, 2001, p.96

Online Articles

http://onstagemag.com/ar/performance_bashing_night_away/index.htm
   (*Onstage*, "Bashing the Night Away," May 2003)

Online Databases

Biography Resource Center Online, 2004, article from *Contemporary Musicians*, 2002

ADDRESS

The Donnas
Atlantic Records
9229 Sunset Boulevard
Los Angeles, CA 90069

WORLD WIDE WEB SITE

http://www.thedonnas.com

Tim Duncan 1976-

American Professional Basketball Player for
the San Antonio Spurs
NBA Most Valuable Player in 2002 and 2003

BIRTH

Victor Theodore Duncan was born on April 25, 1976, on the
island of St. Croix in the United States Virgin Islands, located
in the Caribbean. His father, William Duncan, was a mason
and also operated a hotel and worked at an oil refinery. His
mother, Delysia Bryan Duncan, better known as Ione, worked

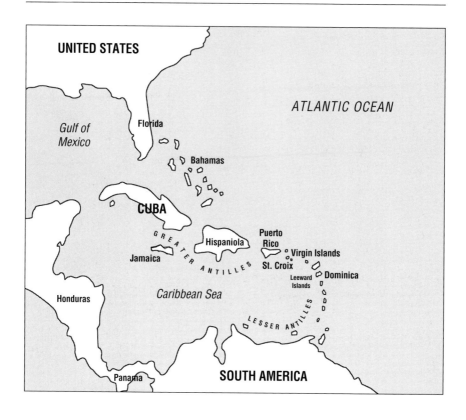

UNITED STATES

ATLANTIC OCEAN

Gulf of
Mexico

Florida

Bahamas

CUBA

Hispaniola
Jamaica
GREATER
ANTILLES

Puerto
Rico
Virgin Islands
St. Croix
Leeward
Islands
Dominica

Honduras

Caribbean Sea

LESSER ANTILLES

Panama

SOUTH AMERICA

as a midwife—a person who assists mothers when they give birth. Tim has two older sisters, Cheryl and Tricia, and three half-brothers, William, John, and Scott.

YOUTH

The Virgin Islands are made up of 100 or so small isles in the Caribbean Sea. They lie about 1,100 miles southeast of Miami, Florida. The United States purchased several of the islands in 1917, including St. Croix—Duncan's home. These became known as the United States (or U.S.) Virgin Islands. This means that Duncan grew up as a United States citizen, even though he lived far away from the U.S. mainland.

In many ways, St. Croix is similar to the United States. It receives many of the same television shows, and kids often dress in T-shirts and shorts. The climate and scenery are quite different, however. Like other islands in the Caribbean, St. Croix is beautiful and tropical. It's surrounded by warm water and has lots of beaches and palm trees. Given these surroundings, it's not surprising that Duncan's first sport was swimming rather than basketball. What is surprising is that he didn't do much of his swimming in the ocean. Duncan was afraid of sharks, so he preferred to swim in pools. Fortunately, that's where the races were held. He began swimming in meets at a young age, following in the wake of his older sisters, who were both strong swimmers. In fact, Tricia was so good that she swam in the 1988 Olympics as a member of the Virgin Islands team.

A big reason for the success of Tim and his siblings was that their parents were very involved in their sporting activities, especially their mother, Ione. She was always there to show her support—and when Ione gave you support, *everybody* heard it. "Every meet she was the loudest parent there," Tim remembered. "Somehow I could always pick out her voice yelling over everybody else." She had a say-

> *Duncan's parents were very involved in their sporting activities, especially his mother, Ione. She was always there to show her support—and when Ione gave you support,* **everybody** *heard it. "Every meet she was the loudest parent there,"* Tim remembered. *"Somehow I could always pick out her voice yelling over everybody else."*

ing that she used to motivate her children: "Good, better, best. Never let it rest. Until your good is better, and your better is best." By the time he was 13 years old, Duncan was getting closer to being the best: he was rated among the top swimmers in the United States in his age group for the 400-meter freestyle. It was thought he might be able to compete in the Olympics as early as the 1992 summer games.

The Storm Hits

Age 13 turned out to be Tim Duncan's unlucky year. A few months after he became a teenager, he was introduced to one of the biggest dangers in the Caribbean: a hurricane. In September 1989, Hurricane Hugo bore down on St. Croix. His family took shelter in their home and hoped for the best. "It was very scary," Duncan recalled in *Tim Duncan: Tower of Power.* "You could hear trees snapping. I had never experienced anything like that." The Duncans' house came through the storm fairly well, but that wasn't true of the rest of island. Roofs were ripped from houses. Boats were tossed onto the land. And the pool where Duncan's swim team trained—the only suitable one on the island—was totally destroyed. His team moved their practices to the ocean. Duncan was still afraid of sharks, and he found it difficult to swim well in the open sea. His interest in the sport began to fade.

But an even worse catastrophe had begun in the months before the hurricane arrived. Duncan's mother had been diagnosed with breast cancer. She began chemotherapy treatments immediately, but they were delayed after the hospital was damaged by the storm. By the following spring her condition had grown worse. In April 1990, the day before Duncan's 14th birthday, she died. Without the woman he called his "number one fan," Duncan became even less interested in swimming, and he gave up the sport. "The hurricane broke Tim's routine by taking away our pool," his sister Tricia said in *Sports Illustrated*. "Then when Mom passed, he lost his motivation."

Fortunately, there was another sport that helped take his mind off his grief. The year before, Tim's sister Cheryl, who had married and moved to Ohio, had sent a basketball hoop and backboard to her brother as a present. His father had set it up, but it wasn't until after Ione's death that Duncan began to concentrate on the game. A big reason for his interest was that Cheryl and her husband, Ricky Lowery, had moved back to St. Croix to help out after Ione had died. Lowery had played college basketball in Ohio, and he began to work with Duncan on the basic skills. "You could just tell this kid was a ballplayer," Lowery later said. "First starting out, he was a bit awkward, but he caught on quickly." Lowery and Duncan spent long hours playing one-on-one games, with Lowery giving Duncan a crash course in hoops. "I wanted to make sure he learned the game right. I spent a lot of time with him on a personal basis, getting him ready for the next level."

>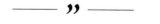
>
> *"You could just tell this kid was a ballplayer. First starting out, he was a bit awkward, but he caught on quickly," said his brother-in-law, Ricky Lowery, a former college player. "I wanted to make sure he learned the game right. I spent a lot of time with him on a personal basis, getting him ready for the next level."*

EDUCATION

When she was alive, Ione Duncan made sure her children applied themselves to their studies as well as their sporting events. Tim's sister Tricia remembers that her brother "used to make high honors all the time" in his schoolwork. He was even allowed to skip a grade during elementary school. As a result, Duncan was a year younger than his classmates from that point on. He began high school at St. Dunstan's Episcopal at age 14, the same year that he took up basketball. Even though he had only been seriously playing the sport for a few months, he made the team.

Duncan's athletic abilities were aided by his height—at age 14 he was already six feet tall and still growing. He played guard during his freshman season. Two years later and nine inches taller (and *still* growing), Duncan was the team's center. Local papers began to cover his games, and he drew the attention of some college recruiters. But few universities hear about promising players in the Caribbean, so only a few schools showed interest in Duncan. Providence College offered him a scholarship, then changed their mind and withdrew it.

Fortunately, a tour of rookie NBA players paid a visit to St. Croix before Duncan's senior year in high school. Duncan got a chance to match up against rising star Alonzo Mourning in a game, and Duncan did very well. News of the performance soon reached Dave Odom, head coach at Wake Forest University in Winston-Salem, North Carolina. Odom soon made a trip to St. Croix and got to see Duncan play in an informal outdoor game. Informal or not, it allowed the Wake Forest coach to see what Duncan could do on the court. He made a scholarship offer, and a month later Duncan accepted. He was about to move from a small Caribbean island to a major university in a large North Carolina city. And he was about to test his skills against the best amateur players in the world.

Duncan attended Wake Forest University from 1993 to 1997. There, he spent time on the basketball court with the Demon Deacons and also spent time in classes, majoring in psychology. Though he wasn't a star student, he maintained a 2.7 grade-point average. He completed his studies in the spring of 1997, earning a bachelor's degree.

CAREER HIGHLIGHTS

Duncan's career really began as a college student at Wake Forest. When he began his first season with the Demon Deacons (1993-94), Coach Odom didn't expect him to play much. But then two other players became ineligible, so Duncan became the starting center. He was certainly big enough to fill the position: during his college years, he reached his full seven-foot height.

During his sophomore year at Wake Forest, Duncan and the Demon Deacons lost to Oklahoma in the NCAA tournament, March 1995.

No one knew much about him at the beginning. Most fans focused on Randolph Childress, Wake Forest's star player. Early in the season, Duncan simply played and learned, but soon he started to show his stuff. He averaged 10 rebounds and almost 10 points a game and set the school record for the number of blocked shots in a season. He had become an important player much sooner than anyone expected. "He has made us a completely different team," Odom said. With Duncan's help Wake Forest made it to the NCAA tournament, but they were eliminated after losing their second game.

Off the court, Duncan settled into life at the university. When he first arrived, many of the people he met had never heard of the Virgin Islands. Sometimes they asked funny questions about Duncan's home. One woman even wondered if people wore clothes on St. Croix. Duncan soon made friends, however, and began to enjoy life in Winston-Salem.

Sophomore Sensation

At the beginning of Duncan's second college season (1994-95), Wake Forest wasn't expected to do well against its rivals in the Atlantic Coast Conference (ACC). But the play of Duncan and Randolph Childress made the Demon Deacons strong contenders. At the close of the regular season, Wake Forest claimed the ACC championship. The team then entered the NCAA tournament, where they won two games before being beaten by Oklahoma State. It had been a surprisingly good year for the team and an amazing year for Duncan. He had upped his numbers, averaging 16.8 points and 12.5 rebounds per game. He also proved himself an outstanding defensive player who could force opponents to alter their attack.

His performance caught the attention of the basketball world. Jerry West, the general manager of the Los Angeles Lakers and former pro superstar, was one of several people who called Duncan the best college player in the country. Suddenly, everyone began to wonder if Duncan would turn professional and move to the National Basketball Association (NBA). Because NBA players can earn enormous amounts of money, many promising college players decide to turn pro before they have completed the full four years of college ball. Duncan, however, wasn't hoping for a big payoff—at least not yet. "To be honest, I'm not looking too far ahead," he explained. "I mean, I've thought about the pros, obviously. But not to the extent that it would happen this year. I'm not going anywhere this year."

He made the same choice one year later, following his junior season. Many people were amazed that Duncan could turn down the millions that the pros were offering, but he had his reasons. The biggest was a vow he had made years before. "I promised my mother when she was dying that I would graduate and I will carry that promise out," he told one journalist. Another factor was his age. Even after three years in college, Duncan was still only 20. "I just felt too young to be in the NBA," he said. "I was not ready." He was also enjoying his time at a student. "The truth is, he loves college," his coach said. "He loves hanging out with people his own age."

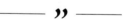

> *Many people were amazed that Duncan could turn down the millions that the pros were offering, but he had his reasons. The biggest was a vow he had made years before. "I promised my mother when she was dying that I would graduate and I will carry that promise out," he told one journalist.*

Taking the Heat

In his junior and senior years, Duncan faced new challenges. After Randolph Childress graduated, Duncan had to become the team's leader. Also, teams were able to double- and triple-team him because they no longer had to worry about the high-scoring Childress. Despite the added pressure, Duncan was able to adjust and improve his game, and his statistics got better and better. He averaged 20.8 points and 14.7 rebounds in his final year.

As he became more famous, Duncan had to deal with greater expectations and more demands from fans and reporters. Many players, especially young ones, have trouble dealing with this attention. Perhaps Duncan did, too, but you would never know it from his behavior. He almost always spoke quietly and appeared calm — even while on the court. His teammates nicknamed him Spock, after the "Star Trek" character who shows no emotion.

Some people mistook his reserved behavior as a sign of boredom and thought that he sometimes wasn't interested in the game. Duncan was well aware that some people criticized his intensity, but — not surprisingly — he didn't get too excited about it. "It's just how I was brought up," he

*Duncan stretches for the ball over Chris Alexander (#30) of the Virginia
Cavaliers, March 1996.*

said. "It's my personality, and it carries onto the court. But I don't see myself as laid back as people say. Once I'm out there, I want to play. I'm excited to play."

Duncan was also excited to win a national championship with Wake Forest, but it was not to be. In his junior year (1995-96), the Demon Deacons won their second consecutive ACC tournament. But their season ended in the NCAA tournament, when the University of Kentucky beat them soundly, 83-63. In his senior year (1996-97), they made it to the second round of the NCAAs but lost to Stanford. Duncan was disappointed with the losses, but he knew he had a big future in front of him. As he left Wake Forest in the spring of 1997, he waited to hear where he was going to play pro ball.

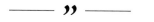

> *Some people mistook Duncan's reserved behavior as a sign of boredom and thought that he sometimes wasn't interested in the game. "It's just how I was brought up," he said. "It's my personality, and it carries onto the court. But I don't see myself as laid back as people say. Once I'm out there, I want to play. I'm excited to play."*

Going Pro

The San Antonio Spurs made Duncan the first choice in the 1997 NBA draft. His initial contract paid him $10 million dollars over three years. In joining the Spurs, he became a teammate of David Robinson, one of the top centers in the NBA. Nicknamed "the Admiral" (because he had attended the U.S. Naval Academy and served in the U.S. Navy), Robinson was a seasoned veteran who had spent seven years in the league. Even before official training began for the 1997-98 season, Robinson invited Duncan to his home in Colorado so that they could start getting ready for the season.

The two talented big men made San Antonio a team to be reckoned with, and Duncan quickly got the attention of his opponents. Following a preseason game against the Houston Rockets, Charles Barkley said that "I have seen the future, . . . and it wears No. 21" — a reference to Duncan's jersey numeral.

Duncan was officially listed as the Spurs' power forward, with Robinson as the center. During their first season together, Robinson gave Duncan pointers on the players he would face each night. Though Robinson was the more experienced NBA player, he admitted that he admired Duncan's maturity and patience. "Tim brings that calm perspective to things," Robinson told *Sports Illustrated*. "You don't often say this about a rookie, but he's got a lot of wisdom." Duncan dismissed such compliments. "I'm a kid. Corny as that sounds, that's what I am." He certainly had his share of toys: when the team went on the road, Duncan carried his own video-game system with him, so he could play in his hotel room.

Nicknamed "The Twin Towers" and "The Swat Team" (for their shot-blocking abilities), Duncan and Robinson made the Spurs into contenders. (The season before Duncan's arrival, with Robinson

Number one — Duncan poses after being selected by the San Antonio Spurs as the first pick overall in the 1997 NBA draft.

injured, the Spurs had won only 20 games.) In the 1998 NBA playoffs, the Spurs were eliminated by the Utah Jazz in the conference semifinals, but the season had been a big success for Duncan. He was named the NBA Schick Rookie of the Year and the *Sporting News* Rookie of the Year, and he was the only first-year player to make the All-Star team.

A Year to Remember

The start of the following season (1998-99) was delayed because of a labor dispute between NBA owners and players. Once games resumed, the Spurs took a few weeks to get themselves together. Then they started winning. Robinson and Duncan honed their attack, with Duncan becoming the higher scorer. The regular season closed with San Antonio winning 31 of their final 36 games. They hit the playoffs in high gear and never slowed down. After winning their series against the Minnesota Timberwolves, the Spurs took on the Los Angeles Lakers, who were led by Shaquille O'Neal and Kobe Bryant. The Spurs took the Lakers apart, sweeping the series in four games. In Game Three, Duncan scored 37 points.

Next, San Antonio swept the Portland Trailblazers to advance to the NBA Finals against the New York Knicks. The series opened in San Antonio, where Duncan put on a show for the hometown fans. He scored 33 points

Duncan grabs a rebound during the NBA finals against the
New York Knicks, June 1999.

on the way to a convincing Spurs win. The rest of the series was pretty much the same. The Knicks managed to win Game Three, but otherwise San Antonio dominated. Duncan was the most dominant of all: he averaged 27.4 points a game in the series. When the buzzer sounded in Game Five, the San Antonio Spurs were the 1999 World Champions. In just his second year in the pros, Duncan had helped lead his team to the top. He was named Most Valuable Player in the Finals and placed third in voting for the season MVP.

Winning and Joking

Duncan had proven himself a winner and one of the best players in the game. Still, sports writers often focused on his apparent lack of emotion. As in his college days, some suggested that he was indifferent—that he didn't care if his team won or lost. Duncan didn't agree with these opinions. In an article for *Sport* magazine that he wrote himself, he explained that his composure was an important part of his game. "Emotions must not always be shown. If you show excitement, then you may also show disappointment or frustration. If your opponent picks up on this frustration, you're at a disadvantage. I make sure my opponents don't know what's going on in my head." His teammates certainly didn't have any problem with Duncan's commitment: "There is nobody more focused or fiercer than Tim when it comes to basketball," said Spurs forward Mario Elie.

———— " ————

"Emotions must not always be shown," Duncan once said in explaining how his composure was an important part of his game. "If you show excitement, then you may also show disappointment or frustration. If your opponent picks up on this frustration, you're at a disadvantage. I make sure my opponents don't know what's going on in my head."

———— " ————

Though he may be very focused on the court, Duncan likes to have fun off of it. "Life is too short to be serious all the time," he wrote. That may explain why he likes to wear his practice shorts backwards and why he likes to play pranks and jokes. Duncan's friend and teammate Antonio Daniels said he is a practical joker but "not a very good one." Daniels also said his friend's jokes were "cheap-shot humor. But it's funny." Will Perdue, another teammate, said that there is definitely one thing that makes Duncan get

Duncan (# 21), Robinson (# 50), and their teammates celebrate after defeating the New York Knicks 78-77 in Game 5 of the NBA Finals, 1999.

excited: "kicking somebody's behind in Sony PlayStation. He does take a lot of pride in that."

Hurting and Healing

As the 1999-2000 season opened, the Spurs had a good chance to repeat as champions. Everything changed on April 11, however. In a late-season game against Sacramento, Duncan tore the cartilage in his knee. It was a serious injury that ended his season. The Spurs had already qualified for the playoffs, but with Duncan on the bench they were eliminated in the first round.

The injury proved doubly disappointing for Duncan because it forced him to withdraw from the U.S. Olympic basketball team that was set to compete in the 2000 summer games in Sydney, Australia. He had played with the national team in previous tournaments and was looking forward to trying for the gold medal that he had dreamed about during his years as a swimmer. In late May, Duncan underwent knee surgery to repair the damaged cartilage, then worked on getting himself back into shape.

On top of everything else, Duncan had a big decision to make in the summer of 2000. His initial contract with San Antonio had ended, and he was now a free agent who could sign with any NBA team. Even with his injury, he was one of the most desirable players in the league. The Orlando Magic did their best to convince Duncan that he should join their team. They flew him and his girlfriend Amy Sherrill to Florida, gave them private tours of Disney World, and introduced them to local resident Tiger Woods. San Antonio wasn't giving up without a fight, though. They did their best to convince Duncan that he should remain a Spur. In the end, Duncan agreed. He re-signed with San Antonio. "Orlando had a lot to offer," he said after making his choice, but he added that "when it came down to it, I just like what I had here."

Teammate Will Perdue said that there is definitely one thing that makes Duncan get excited: "kicking somebody's behind in Sony PlayStation. He does take a lot of pride in that."

It took some time for Duncan to get back in top form after his injury. By the second half of the 2000-01 season, however, he was again one of the best in the league. In the regular season, the Spurs won more games than any other team in the NBA and had hopes of regaining their championship. Then, in the Western Conference Finals, they met the Los Angeles Lakers. Over the previous two years, the Lakers had become the most powerful team in the league and had won the NBA crown the previous season. The Lakers finished off the Spurs in four straight games, bringing San Antonio's season to a disappointing close.

Talking and Teaching

The Spurs were forced to make some adjustments the following season (2001-02). David Robinson was burdened by injuries and struggled with his performance. This put more pressure on Duncan, both as a player and as the team's leader. He responded to both challenges. Spurs forward Malik Rose remarked that "this season [Duncan's] always talking, teaching, communicating. He's always trying to get us pumped up." Duncan also had one of his best years as a performer, scoring an amazing 2,089 points and hauling down 1,042 rebounds.

As the team entered the playoffs, Robinson was out of the lineup with a strained back. Then, in the midst of the Spurs' first-round series against Seattle, Duncan faced a new challenge. His father died at age 71, after battling cancer for several years. Duncan flew to St. Croix to be with his family. This caused him to miss one playoff game—a game that the Spurs lost. Upon his return, however, they won the final game of the series to advance to the next round. There, the defending champion Lakers awaited them once again. The teams split the first two games, but then Los Angeles took control. The Lakers finished off the Spurs, then went on to claim their third championship. Duncan's great season hadn't gone unnoticed, however. He was named the NBA's most valuable player in 2002.

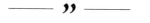

> *"Dave has taught me a lot about being a being a leader, being a winner, and about doing things the right way, with some dignity,"* Duncan said of his friend and teammate. *"I have been very fortunate to have been able to play with him from the beginning."*

The Admiral's Last Voyage

David Robinson announced that the 2002-03 season would be his last. After a long and distinguished career, the injuries were catching up with him. Still, he was expected to be a valuable asset for the Spurs in his final year, and he had certainly been an influence on Duncan's development as a professional player. "Dave has taught me a lot about being a being a leader, being a winner, and about doing things the right way, with some dignity," Duncan said of his friend and teammate. "I have been very fortunate to have been able to play with him from the beginning."

To make the Admiral's last voyage a memorable one, the Spurs played some great basketball. They finished the regular season with 60 wins, tying Dallas for the best record in the league. In the playoffs, the Spurs dispatched the Phoenix Suns, then squared off against the Lakers once more. This time, things were different. With the series even at two games apiece, Duncan scored 27 points in Game Five to put San Antonio up three games to two. In Game Six he was even better, scoring 37. The Spurs sent the

Robinson and Duncan pause for a hug in the closing minutes of the Spurs 88-77 win over the New Jersey Nets, June 2003.

Lakers packing and moved on to the Western Conference Finals, where they beat the Dallas Mavericks four games to two.

That brought the team to the NBA Finals, where their opponents were the New Jersey Nets. It was a tough defensive series marked by low scores and missed shots. While most of the other players struggled to put points on the board, Duncan was as consistent as usual: he averaged 24.2 points a game. The Spurs battled to a three-games-to-two advantage in the series. With a win in Game Six, they could become champions, but the game was a tough one. They found themselves trailing by nine points with only nine minutes to go. Then, in a thrilling rally, they scored 14 unanswered points and put the Nets away. Duncan had his second NBA Championship in five years and his second series MVP award. Also, for the second year in a row he was voted the most valuable player in the NBA. Yet another honor came in December 2003, when Duncan and David Robinson were named Sportsmen of the Year by *Sports Illustrated*.

Going for Gold

Following the 2002-03 season, Duncan was again eligible to become a free agent. This time, however, there was less indecision about staying with the Spurs. He inked a seven-year deal with San Antonio worth $122 million. With his pro future settled, Duncan could concentrate on playing basketball on a different level: he joined Team USA at a qualifying tournament in Puerto Rico, where the team earned the right to participate in the 2004 Olympics. Barring another injury, Duncan will get his shot at a gold medal at the summer games in Athens.

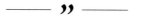

> *If Duncan bragged about his abilities more, some say, he could be a bigger star. Duncan refuses to play that part. "Everything I do is basic, and that doesn't sell," he claimed. "I don't have the icing. My icing is, I just want to win."*

Whether or not he wins gold, Duncan is recognized as one of the top players in the NBA and has even earned comparisons to such legends as Michael Jordan. Many sports writers have suggested that he may be too quiet for his own good. If he bragged about his abilities more, some say, he could be a bigger star. Duncan refuses to play that part. "Everything I do is basic, and that doesn't sell," he claimed. "I don't have the icing. My icing is, I just want to win."

MARRIAGE AND FAMILY

Duncan married his longtime girlfriend Amy Sherrill on July 21, 2001. The two had met when they were students at Wake Forest, where Sherrill had majored in health and exercise sciences. They have two Labrador retrievers, Zen and Shadoe, and a cockapoo named Nicole.

HOBBIES AND OTHER INTERESTS

Duncan has been a video-game fanatic for many years. He also likes to watch movies and surf the Internet. Another of his hobbies is collecting knives and swords. He's especially proud of the Japanese samurai sword that he owns. Both Duncan and his wife, Amy, spend a lot of time raising

money for charities. Some of this work is carried out through the Tim Duncan Foundation, an organization that provides funding to non-profit groups in education, health, and youth sports. Amy serves as the foundation's executive vice president. They also raise money to fight against the two diseases that claimed Duncan's parents—breast cancer and prostrate cancer. He and Amy host a celebrity-bowling event each year with the proceeds going to a variety of cancer-related causes.

HONORS AND AWARDS

NCAA Defensive Player of the Year: 1994-97
NABC National Defensive Player of the Year: 1995-1997

College Basketball Player of the Year: 1996-97

Associated Press All America First Team: 1997

Associated Press National Player of the Year: 1997

John R. Wooden Award for Outstanding College Basketball Player in the United States (Los Angeles Athletic Club): 1997

Naismith Basketball Award for Men's College Player of the Year (Atlanta Tipoff Club): 1997

National Association of Basketball Coaches National Player of the Year: 1997

U.S. Basketball Writers National Player of the Year: 1997

All NBA First Team: 1998-2003

NBA All-Rookie First Team: 1998

NBA Schick Rookie of the Year: 1998

NBA All Star: 1998, 2000-2003

Sporting News Rookie of the Year: 1998

NBA All-Defensive First Team: 1999-2003

NBA Finals Most Valuable Player: 1999, 2003

NBA All-Star Game Co-Most Valuable Player: 2000

NBA Most Valuable Player: 2002, 2003

IBM Award: 2002, for all-around contribution to team's success

Basketball Digest Player of the Year: 2001-2002

Sporting News Player of the Year: 2001-2002 and 2002-2003.

Sports Illustrated Sportsman of the Year: 2003 (co-winner with David Robinson)

USA Basketball Male Athlete of the Year: 2003

FURTHER READING

Books

Byman, Jeremy. *Great Athletes: Tim Duncan*, 2000
Contemporary Black Biography, Vol. 20, 1998
Sports Stars, Series 5, 1999
Stewart, Mark. *Tim Duncan: Tower of Power*, 1999
Who's Who among African Americans, 2003

Periodicals

Basketball Digest, Summer 2002, p.26
Current Biography Yearbook, 1999
Los Angeles Times, Dec. 6, 1995, p.C1; Nov. 13, 1997, p.C1
New York Times, June 25, 1996, p.B15; Mar. 31, 1998, p.C2; June 20, 1999, sec. 8, p.3

Philadelphia Inquirer, Mar. 22, 1995, p.D1
Sport, July 1997, p.34; Mar. 1999, p.34; Oct. 1999, p.86
Sporting News, June 23, 2003, p.10; Nov. 10, 2003, p.20
Sports Illustrated, Nov. 27, 1995, p.78; Feb. 17, 1997, p.28; Nov. 24, 1997, p.58; May 31, 1999, p.48; July 7, 1999, p.77; May 20, 2002, p.42; Dec. 15, 2003, pp.58 and 66
USA Today, Jan. 29, 2003, p.C1
Washington Post, Jan. 13, 1996, p.F1

Online Databases

Biography Resource Center Online, 2004, articles from *Contemporary Black Biography*, 1998; *Sports Stars*, 1999; and *Who's Who among African Americans*, 2003

ADDRESS

Tim Duncan
San Antonio Spurs
One SBC Center
San Antonio, TX 78219

WORLD WIDE WEB SITES

http://www.nba.com
http://www.slamduncan.com

Shirin Ebadi 1947-

Iranian Lawyer and Human Rights Advocate
Winner of the 2003 Nobel Peace Prize

BIRTH

Shirin Ebadi (pronounced shih-REEN eh-BAH-dee) was born
in 1947 in the town of Hamadan, 180 miles southwest of Tehran, the capital of Iran. Her mother was Minu (sometimes
spelled Mino or Minoo) Yamini (also listed as Amidi), and her
father was Muhammad-Ali Ebadi, a lawyer and law professor.
She has a brother named Jafar. Ebadi grew up speaking the

Farsi language, also known as Persian, which is written in the Arabic alphabet. When words are translated from Farsi to English, there can be several different spellings.

BACKGROUND ON IRAN

Ebadi was certainly affected by the many changes her country experienced throughout the 1900s. Once known as Persia, Iran has long been an important and influential part of the Middle East. The discovery of the country's vast oil reserves in the early 1900s made it even more important. World powers such as Russia, Great Britain, and the United States all kept a close eye on events in Iran. All of them wanted to have access to its rich resources.

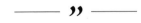

Historically, women faced many restrictions in Iran. For instance, they did not leave their homes very often, and when they did, they were expected to keep their faces covered with a veil. Very few women got an education or held jobs outside the home. These restrictions were found in many countries in the Islamic world in the early 1900s and even today.

Another important factor in Iran's history is that it is an Islamic country—most people are Muslims who follow the religion of Islam. Up until the early 1900s, Muslim religious figures, or clerics, were very powerful because they administered the laws of the country. In fact, Ebadi's grandfather was a religious judge.

The Pahlavis and Modern Iran

This system changed in the 1920s, after Reza Shah Pahlavi took control of the country in a military coup. This began the long reign of the Pahlavi dynasty. Reza Shah himself ruled Iran until 1941, and his son, Muhammad Reza Shah Pahlavi, ruled from 1941 to 1979. The Pahlavis introduced modern, Western-style laws and reduced the influence of the Muslim clerics in the areas of education and legal proceedings. Iran remained an Islamic country, but religious figures had less say in governmental and social policy.

The Pahlavis made other changes, as well. Previously, women had faced many restrictions. For instance, they did not leave their homes very often, and when they did, they were expected to keep their faces covered with a veil. Very few women got an education or held jobs outside the home. These restrictions were found in many countries in the Islamic world in the

105

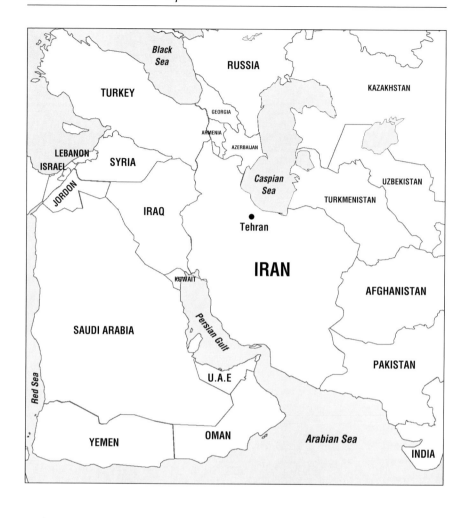

early 1900s, and some nations still observe these practices today. Some Muslims—though certainly not all of them—believe that women should not have a large public role in society. They interpret certain passages in the Koran (the Muslim holy book) to mean that women should be subservient to men and that women should keep their faces and bodies well covered when away from home.

The Pahlavis discouraged these practices. Under their rule, girls were allowed to attend school and women were allowed more freedom in where they went and what they wore. This made Iran one of the most progressive countries in the Middle East. While the Pahlavis introduced some social freedoms, they did not promote political freedom. Both father and son were absolute rulers who crushed political dissent.

EBADI'S YOUTH

Under the Shah, Ebadi's father, Muhammad-Ali Ebadi, became a well-respected figure in Iran's modernized legal system. He wrote a famous textbook on commercial law that is still in print. At the time of Shirin's birth, the family lived in Hamadan, but when she was six months old, they moved to Tehran, the capital and largest city in Iran.

In the early 1960s, when Ebadi was a teenager, new laws were passed that gave women even more freedom. They won the right to vote and to hold political office, and they gained greater rights in attaining divorces (though still less than those granted to men). It also became more common for women to drive cars and hold jobs. While such freedoms are taken for granted in many countries, they are rare in parts of the Islamic world. Even today, such countries as Saudi Arabia enforce strict rules that prevent women from traveling by themselves or even speaking with a man to whom they are not related.

> *In the early 1960s, when Ebadi was a teenager, new laws were passed that gave women more freedom. They won the right to vote and to hold political office, and they gained greater rights in attaining divorces.*

EDUCATION

The 1960s were also a time when large numbers of Iranian women began attending universities. When she was old enough, Ebadi joined them. She enrolled at the University of Tehran and studied law, following in her father's footsteps. She graduated with her degree in 1971.

CAREER HIGHLIGHTS

Becoming a Judge

After finishing school, Ebadi quickly became an important figure in the legal system. In 1975, just four years after leaving the university, she became the first female judge in Iran. Her official title was President of the City Court of Tehran. Other women soon assumed important judicial positions throughout the country. With such moves, the government of Muhammad Reza Shah Pahlavi showed that it was still dedicated to expanding the rights of women.

But by the late 1970s, the Shah's government was in trouble. Many Iranians were opposed to the lack of political freedom. In addition, conservative religious figures resented the liberal social reforms instituted by the Pahlavis. In late 1978, the events began to unfold that became known as the Iranian Revolution. Widespread demonstrations, strikes, and riots took place throughout the country. Unable to restore order, the Shah left the country in January 1979. A Muslim opposition leader, Ayatollah Ruhollah Khomeini, returned to Iran and played a key role in establishing a new government. In April 1979, the Islamic Republic of Iran was established.

From Judge to Clerk

In the beginning, Ebadi supported the revolution. She joined the strike committee of the Ministry of Justice and hoped the nation's new government would make Iran a place of greater political and legal freedoms. But that was not to be. The new government became dominated by Muslims who favored a very conservative form of Islamic belief. Sometimes known as "hard-liners," these figures favored more power for religious clerics. They also set about repealing some of the country's progressive reforms — especially those that granted more freedom for women.

Ebadi was soon notified that she could no longer be a judge. She was told that women were too emotional to be deciding legal cases. She was instead given the lowly rank of legal assistant and forced to perform clerical duties at the Ministry of Justice. She later compared this experience to that of making "the president of a university into a janitor."

Over the next few years, the government enacted more legal and social changes that fit its conservative vision. In seeking to undo some of the reforms of the pre-revolutionary period, the powerful religious clerics passed a number of laws that gave men certain privileges in the legal system. The hard-liners also turned against foreign powers that had supported the Shah, especially the United States. The government's anti-American sentiment inspired a group of radical Iranian students to seize the U.S. embassy in Tehran in late 1979. They took 52 Americans as hostages and held them for more than a year.

A Proud Iranian

Many Iranians who did not agree with the conservative reforms chose to leave the country. Ebadi was not happy with being removed as judge, and she did not like the loss of political and social freedoms then taking place. Still, she decided to remain in Iran. As she explained in an article in *The Times* (London, England), "I'm proud to be Iranian and I'll live in my country as long as I can."

After finishing school, Ebadi quickly became an important figure in the legal system. In 1975, just four years after leaving the university, she became the first female judge in Iran. Her official title was President of the City Court of Tehran.

Ebadi continued to work at the Ministry of Justice until 1984, when she was given the opportunity to take an early retirement. She then joined a law firm, but her involvement in legal cases could only go so far: at that time, women lawyers were prevented from performing many duties. Still, she continued to work on legal issues: she began teaching law at Tehran University and served as a consultant to businesses.

In the early 1990s, women were again allowed to work as fully practicing lawyers, so Ebadi opened her own law office. This allowed her to use her legal skills to help those she felt were being mistreated by the Iranian justice system. She soon became well known for defending the rights of women and children. Because many of her clients were poor, she often received no pay for her work.

Fighting the System

Several of Ebadi's cases focused public attention on laws that had been enacted since the 1979 revolution. For instance, the Iranian legal code considers the life of a male to be twice as valuable as the life of a female. Also, in many cases the divorce laws automatically give the father custody of children, regardless of other circumstances. There is even an Iranian law that states that a father can't be convicted of murdering his children. Ebadi's court battles didn't succeed in changing these laws, but they did make Iranians more aware of the extreme measures sponsored by the hard-liners. "All these laws were written after the 1979 revolution," she explained. The conservatives who wrote the laws intended to promote Islamic values, but Ebadi believes that they were misguided. "The problem is that our laws come from a wrong interpretation of Islam," she said.

> The Iranian legal code includes many laws that place a higher value on men than on women. "All these laws were written after the 1979 revolution," she explained. The conservatives who wrote the laws intended to promote Islamic values, but Ebadi believes that they were misguided. "The problem is that our laws come from a wrong interpretation of Islam," she said.

In addition to her court cases, Ebadi established the Society for the Protection of the Rights of the Child, an organization that pursues a range of child-welfare issues. She also wrote books. Some focused attention on the mistreatment of children; others addressed Iran's record on human rights. Like many others around the world, Ebadi believes that there are certain rights that every human is entitled to, including democracy, equal treatment under the law, and freedom of speech.

Also, she feels that religion — including her own Islamic faith — should not be used as a reason to deny basic human rights. She has often stated her belief that "there is no difference between Islam and human rights." By this she means that one can faithfully follow the Muslim religion and still uphold such ideals as equal rights. In her opinion, those Muslims that take a more extreme view — claiming men are superior to women, for instance — are misreading the Koran.

Ebadi is shown speaking below portraits of Iran's leaders (left to right):
Mohammad Khatami, President of Iran; Ayatollah Ruhollah Khomeini,
the late founder of the Islamic Republic of Iran; and his successor,
Ayatollah Ali Khamenei, Supreme Leader of Iran.

Deadly Politics

By the late 1990s it appeared that a growing number of Iranians opposed the hard-liners. In 1997, Mohammad Khatami was elected president. Though he is a Muslim cleric, Khatami is part of the reform movement in Iran. The reformers seek to undo the more extreme laws put in place by the conservatives. In winning his victory, Khatami received a lot of votes from women, many of whom felt that they were being treated unfairly by the country's laws. As Ebadi often points out, women play a very important role in Iranian society. More women than men attend Iranian universities, and women account for three out of every ten workers in the country. Khatami and other reform-minded politicians have continued to receive a lot of support from Iranian voters. The majority of elected officials in Iran's parliament are reformers.

Yet the reformers have not had a lot of success in changing things in Iran. This is because the Iranian political system is not completely controlled by elected officials. There are many powerful figures who are not chosen by voters, and many of them are hard-line conservatives. The most powerful is Ayatollah Ali Khamenei, the country's Supreme Leader. In addition, con-

Ebadi is shown here with a representation of the scales of justice.

servatives exert a lot of control over the country's justice system and the powerful Guardians Council. After President Khatami's election, the struggle between the conservatives and the reformers intensified. The battle soon turned deadly.

In 1998, a number of reformers were beaten, kidnaped, and killed by conservative vigilante groups. Ebadi became involved in the case of a husband and wife who had been stabbed to death in their home. Both were outspoken critics of the hard-liners. While conducting her investigation, she was contacted by two men who said they had been members of a vigilante group. More importantly, the men said that the attacks had been ordered by hard-line politicians. This was startling news because it linked the attack to conservative members of the Iranian government. Ebadi videotaped the men's confessions, then gave the tape to the government. Later, the tape was widely distributed in Iran and caused a political scandal that forced a high-ranking government official to resign.

In 1999 the political turmoil led to student riots in which several people were killed. Again, Ebadi got involved. She represented the family of one of the protestors who died in the riots and called for a thorough investigation of events surrounding the disturbances.

Dangerous Work

Ebadi soon learned that her work could get her in trouble. In 2000, she was charged with insulting public officials. This accusation was caused by her involvement in the videotaped confessions of the vigilantes. Ebadi denied that she had done anything wrong, but she was arrested and held in Evin Prison in Tehran. Evin Prison is infamous because many of those who are jailed for opposing the Iranian government are held there. Some have died under mysterious circumstances while in custody. Ebadi was placed in solitary confinement, and she found the conditions very difficult. She suffered from extreme back pain while locked up but did her best not to show her jailers any weakness. "I try not to complain," she later wrote. After three weeks, Ebadi was released from the prison, but she still had to face the charges in court. She was convicted in a closed hearing and was banned from practicing law for five years. This sentence was later suspended.

Ebadi's jail term and temporary ban showed that her work carried some real risks. But there was an even larger danger: someone might try to kill her. This became very clear when her name appeared on a list of political enemies compiled by the Iranian Intelligence Ministry. It showed that some members of the government considered her a serious threat. Despite the danger, Ebadi continued her work. "Any person who pursues human rights in Iran must live with fear," she said. "It comes to you like hunger, you don't have a choice. But I have learned [to] not let it interfere with my work." Her husband, quoted in *Time*, confirmed that she was aware of the threats: "She was worried, but she didn't let that stop her. . . . She is very brave."

In the early 2000s, Ebadi found new ways to further the cause of human rights. She joined with other activists to establish the Center for the Defense of Human Rights. The organization provides legal help for families of journalists and students who had been imprisoned for speaking out against the government. She also continued to make public speeches and to attend human-rights conferences. In October 2003 she went to Paris, France, to attend a conference on Iranian films and human rights. When it was over, she prepared to return to Iran. But before she left she received a telephone call with some big news.

> ——— " ———
>
> *"Any person who pursues human rights in Iran must live with fear," Ebadi said. "It comes to you like hunger, you don't have a choice. But I have learned not [to] let it interfere with my work."* Her husband, quoted in **Time**, *confirmed that she was aware of the threats: "She was worried, but she didn't let that stop her. . . . She is very brave."*
>
> ——— " ———

The Nobel Peace Prize

The caller informed Ebadi that she had won the Nobel Peace Prize. "I'm shocked," she said shortly after receiving the news. Later, in an interview with Amir Taheri in the *Weekly Standard*, she stated that "I did not even know my name had been put forward for a Nobel." Among the most prestigious awards in the world, the Nobel Prizes are awarded annually in a number of fields, including economics, literature, physics, chemistry, and physiology or medicine. The Peace Prize is awarded to a person or persons who has made a significant contribution to world peace, usually through politics or diplomacy. Ebadi's win was a surprise to many observers — Pope John Paul II had been considered the most likely person to win the prize in 2003. In the official announcement, the Nobel Committee (based in Norway) commended Ebadi:

> As a lawyer, judge, lecturer, writer, and activist, she has spoken out clearly and strongly in her country, Iran, and far beyond its borders. She has stood up as a sound professional, a courageous person, and has never heeded the threats to her own safety. . . . . Ebadi is a conscious Moslem. She sees no conflict between Islam and fundamental human rights. It is important to her that the dialogue between the different cultures and religions of the world should take as its point of departure their shared values. It is a pleasure for the Norwegian Nobel Committee to award the Peace Prize to a woman who is part of the Moslem world, and of whom that world can be proud — along with all who fight for human rights wherever they live.

—————— " ——————

"It's not easy to be a woman today in Iran, because they have laws that are against the rights of women. . . . This prize gives me the energy to continue my fight." In an interview with Norwegian television reporters, Ebadi called the award "very good for human rights in Iran, especially for children's rights in Iran. I hope I can be useful."

—————— " ——————

In addition to giving Ebadi worldwide acclaim, the prize offered money: the Nobel committee awarded her $1.3 million, which will be a big help in furthering her work. She was the first Iranian and only the 11th woman to receive the prize in its 102-year history. She was also the first woman from the Muslim world to win this prestigious award.

After hearing the news, Ebadi delayed her return to Iran and remained in Paris so that she could field questions from reporters. At her first press conference she said "it's not easy to be a woman today in Iran, because they have laws that are against the rights of women. . . . This prize gives me the energy to continue my fight." In an interview with Norwegian television reporters, she called the award "very good for human rights in Iran, especially for children's rights in Iran. I hope I can be useful."

A Controversial Winner

The Paris press conference became a source of controversy. In Iran, when women appear in public they are forced to wear a *roosari*, a type of head covering. But at the Paris press conference, Ebadi was bareheaded. Upon seeing the tape, conservative observers in Iran complained that she wasn't a devout Muslim. Ebadi later explained that she obeys the laws of Iran while in Iran but not elsewhere. In the *Weekly Standard* interview, she commented that "instead of telling girls to cover their hair, we should teach them to use their heads."

Ebadi poses with her Nobel Peace Prize diploma.

Iranian hard-liners had more to complain about. They were unhappy that one of their most vocal critics had received such a prestigious award, so they argued that the Nobel was made for "political" reasons. They suggested that the Norwegian judges had chosen Ebadi because the Europeans wanted to embarrass Iran's devout Muslim leaders. Such reaction from Iranian conservatives was expected, but observers were more surprised when President Khatami, a moderate politician, also downplayed the award. "The Nobel Peace Prize is not very important," the president told a journalist, "the ones that count are the scientific and literary prizes." Khatami also warned Ebadi that she shouldn't let anyone "exploit her success." These comments were viewed as proof that the president was afraid to congratulate Ebadi for fear of angering the conservatives.

A Hero's Welcome

Perhaps the president wasn't excited about Ebadi's prize, but other Iranians certainly were. When she flew back to Tehran a few days after the award was announced, thousands of supporters greeted her at the airport. The majority of them were women, and many of them wore white *roosaris* in opposition to the black scarves preferred by the authorities. "This prize

Ebadi gives her Nobel Peace Prize lecture, 2003.

is not only for me, but for all those in favor of peace, democracy, human rights, and legality," Ebadi told the crowd. At a press conference a short time later, she said that the Nobel "put a heavy burden on my shoulders," but she had her own warning for those that oppose her: "I will not reduce my activities, I will increase them."

Ebadi also had a message for foreign governments that seek changes in Iran. While she is in favor of reforming her country's government, she insists that Iranians direct the changes. "The fight for human rights is conducted in Iran by the Iranian people, and we are against any foreign intervention in Iran." Her comments were aimed primarily at the United States, which had invaded neighboring Iraq in March 2003. Some people believe that the U.S. will put more political pressure on Iran and may even threaten military force. That is something that Ebadi clearly opposes. "America should not interfere in the domestic affairs of any country, including Iran," she said in an interview. "America should be aware that human rights cannot be exported with bombs and bullets."

> "America should not interfere in the domestic affairs of any country, including Iran," Ebadi said in an interview. "America should be aware that human rights cannot be exported with bombs and bullets."

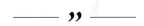

Ebadi is also against violence by Iranians, including violent protests against the government. "There can be no place for disturbances or rioting or destruction," she said. Instead, she seeks peaceful change. Some of her supporters felt that the best way to achieve such a change was to make Ebadi into a politician. They began urging her to seek public office, telling her that she now had enough prestige to lead an opposition political party. Ebadi refused. "I never want to be or will be part of government," she said. "I will always be what I have been—a defender and spokesperson for the weak."

New Challenges

In early November 2003, Ebadi announced that she would assist in a new court case. It involves the death of Zahra Kazemi, a Canadian photojournalist of Iranian descent. Kazemi had gone to Tehran to work on a story about the Iranian justice system. She was arrested for taking photographs outside Evin Prison and then died from a blow to the head while in custody. Her family is seeking to punish those responsible.

117

*Ebadi celebrates with her daughter, Narguess Tavassolian,
who is a law student in Tehran.*

In early 2004, as the country prepared for parliamentary elections, a new political controversy erupted. Hard-line government officials banned thousands of reform candidates who were seeking office, declaring them unsuitable because they did not respect Islam and the Iranian constitution. With the reformers off the ballot, the conservatives won many seats and became the majority party in Parliament. Many Iranians believed that banning reform candidates was unfair. Ebadi was one of many who protested the action by refusing to take part in the voting. "Human rights don't have any meaning without democracy," she said. "Democracy is also based on free elections. And free elections means you can vote for anyone you want to."

Ebadi has received death threats since winning the Nobel, and bodyguards have been assigned to help protect her. Still, she remains dedicated to her mission. She believes that new reforms will take place in Iran because the country is ready for them. "In every society there comes a time when people want to be free," she said in the *Sunday Times* (London). "That time has come in Iran." She feels her Nobel Prize will help inspire others who seek change. "The prize will give more confidence to people who support democracy and human rights. More people will want to join the struggle. And whenever a majority demands change, change will happen."

MARRIAGE AND FAMILY

Ebadi is married to Javed Tavassolian, an electrical engineer. She has two daughters: Negar, who is doing post-graduate work in engineering in Montreal, Canada, and Narguess, who is studying law in Tehran.

WRITINGS

The Rights of the Child: A Study of the Legal Aspects of Children's Rights in Iran, 1994 (nonfiction)
History and Documentation of Human Rights in Iran, 2000 (nonfiction)

—— " ——

"The prize will give more confidence to people who support democracy and human rights. More people will want to join the struggle. And whenever a majority demands change, change will happen."

—— " ——

HONORS AND AWARDS

Human Rights Watch Award: 1996
Rafto Prize (Thorolf Rafto Foundation for Human Rights): 2001
Nobel Peace Prize: 2003, "for her efforts for democracy and human rights"

FURTHER READING

Periodicals

Baltimore Sun, Jan. 28, 1998, p.A1
Christian Science Monitor, Oct. 15, 1999, p.1; Oct. 17, 2003, p.11; Dec. 12, 2003, p.1
Guardian (London), Oct. 11, 2003, p.21; Oct. 13, 2003, p.17; Oct. 15, 2003, p.16
Independent (London), Dec. 24, 1997, p.8; Oct. 11, 2003, p.5
International Herald Tribune (Paris), Oct. 11, 2003, pp.1 and 7
Maclean's, Nov. 17, 2003, p.81
New York Times, Oct. 11, 2003, pp.A1 and A6; Dec. 11, 2003, p.A20
Time, Oct. 20, 2003, p.39
The Times (London), Oct. 11, 2003, pp.7 and 29
San Francisco Chronicle, Oct. 29, 2003, p.A2
Seattle Times, Dec. 1, 1996, p.A25
Sunday Times (London), Oct. 19, 2003, p.7
Washington Post, Nov. 22, 1996, p.A42
Weekly Standard, Nov. 3, 2003, p.22

Other

60 Minutes, "Iran versus Iran, May 10, 1998 (transcript of television broadcast)
All Things Considered, "Hope That the Awarding of the Nobel Peace Prize to
an Iranian Human Rights Activist Will Revitalize the Reform Movement
Inside the Country," Nov. 5, 2003 (transcript of radio broadcast)

ADDRESS

Shirin Ebadi
Iranian Children's Rights Society
PMB #220
27881 La Paz, Suite G.
Laguna Niguel, CA 92677

Shirin Ebadi
Law Firm of Shirin Ebadi
No. 19 Street 57
Seied Jamal eldin Asad Abadi Ave.
Tehran 14349, Iran

WORLD WIDE WEB SITE

http://www.nobel.se

Ashton Kutcher 1978-

American Actor and Producer
Stars in the Fox TV Sitcom "That '70s Show" and
Produced and Starred in the MTV Reality Show
"Punk'd"

BIRTH

Christopher Ashton Kutcher was born on February 7, 1978, in Cedar Rapids, Iowa. Known as Chris to his family and friends, he was born five minutes before his fraternal twin, Michael. Chris was born healthy, but Michael spent his first three months in an incubator and was diagnosed with mild cerebral palsy, a disability caused by damage to the brain at the time of birth.

The twins completed the family of Larry and Diane Kutcher, who already had a three-year-old daughter, Tausha. Larry and Diane supported their family by working on factory assembly lines. Larry worked on the Fruit Roll-Ups assembly line for General Mills, and Diane worked on the Head & Shoulders shampoo line for Procter & Gamble. Larry and Diane divorced in 1991, but they didn't let their differences affect their children. Kutcher praised his parents, saying "My parents are so cool. They couldn't have handled it better."

YOUTH

Not long after his parents' divorce, Kutcher's brother, Michael, nearly died at age 13. Michael suffered from cardiomyopathy, a viral infection of the heart that can be fatal, and he received a heart transplant. During the critical hours before his transplant, Kutcher never left his brother's side. "We fought and argued all the time as kids, but after [the transplant] we bonded completely and we're the best of friends," Kutcher said. His brother became a huge source for his drive in life. "After seeing all that he went through, there's no mountain I can't climb. His courage is really inspirational and brought me very close to God and my spirituality. It's not something that you want to experience, but we all got the best out of it."

Chris has always been the more lively of the twins. High school acquaintance Joy Janda Curfman once said that "What Chris has, Mike lacks. . . . Chris was always the class clown, he wanted a lot of attention, and he got it. He always acted off the wall and did crazy stuff." But after Michael's heart transplant, Chris's antics became "at some level . . . a way of lightening the mood with his brother," Curfman added.

> "We fought and argued all the time as kids, but after [the transplant], we bonded completely and we're the best of friends," Kutcher said about his brother, Michael. "After seeing all that he went through, there's no mountain I can't climb. His courage is really inspirational and brought me very close to God and my spirituality. It's not something that you want to experience, but we all got the best out of it."

Kutcher's love of attention led him to try out for a junior high school play. He loved the stage and discovered that he "got such an adrenaline rush when I was onstage. I felt like a rock star." He played the thief in the seventh-grade production of *The Crying Princess and the Golden Goose*. The experience set in motion Kutcher's desire to be a movie star, and he continued to act in plays and musicals throughout his school years.

In 1993 Diane moved with her children from Cedar Rapids to Homestead, Iowa, a small farming community with a population of 100. There she built a house on a 300-acre farm with Mark Portwood, a construction worker whom she married in 1996. After the move, Kutcher dove head first into school activities. He played football, ran track, wrestled, sang in the jazz choir, joined the science, thespian, and Spanish clubs, and was a member of the National Honor Society. After school hours he and his friends made their own fun, horsing around together in Iowa's vast, remote cornfields. Kutcher especially liked hunting and racing snowmobiles.

> *Joy Janda Curfman, a high school acquaintance, once said that "Chris was always the class clown, he wanted a lot of attention, and he got it. He always acted off the wall and did crazy stuff." But after Michael's heart transplant, Chris's antics became "at some level . . . a way of lightening the mood with his brother."*

But small-town life also included a lot of plain hard work. Kutcher learned from an early age the value of hard work and eagerly sought out jobs for extra money. He spent a lot of his time with animals, especially herding cattle with wranglers. He noted that "When you live in the country you can always find something to do. So you kind of pop from job to job, whether it's cutting the nuts off cattle one day or baling hay the next." To earn money during the winter Kutcher skinned deer at a local butcher shop when he was 17. "That was really crappy," he recalled. "It was really cold and I had to work outside so the meat would stay frozen. Plus you had to spray the deer down with a hose, so you'd wind up completely soaked, and then your clothes would freeze."

Costly Mistakes

Kutcher admits to having made some mistakes in his teens. One particularly stupid stunt involved his arrest at age 18. One night, after saying goodnight to his girlfriend and her father, who was the high school principal, Kutcher and his cousin broke into their high school. Police apprehended them by 3:00 a.m. Kutcher found himself in police custody and in the difficult position of having to explain himself to his girlfriend's father and his own family. He spent the night in a jail cell because his stepfather refused to pay his bail.

A felony charge of third-degree burglary was placed on his record. Although his crime could have carried a jail sentence, Kutcher instead was sentenced to 180 hours of community service and three years of probation. The stunt also cost him his girlfriend and a lead role in the high school production of *Annie,* for which he had already shaved his head in preparation for his part as Daddy Warbucks. His criminal record haunted him years later when the requirements of his probation forced him to plead with a judge to leave Iowa in order to pursue a modeling career. By 2003 Kutcher's record had been expunged, or erased; he was no longer a felon and could finally vote.

>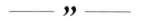
>
> *Kutcher dreamed of becoming a professional actor, but he had real doubts about his abilities. "I was never the star of my high-school plays. My private feeling was, 'You can't even get the lead when there are 52 people in your class. How are you possibly going to go to Hollywood?'"*

EDUCATION

Despite his troubles with the law during his senior year, Kutcher finished high school in 1996 and entered the University of Iowa as a biochemical engineering student. Although he still wanted to become an actor, he had no idea how to make his dream come true. "I realized that unless I left for California, there wasn't anywhere for me to go with the acting. I couldn't afford to move that far, so I decided to go to school and become a genetic engineer." His interest in biochemical engineering was based on his concern for the health of his twin brother; he wanted to find a cure for cardiomyopathy, the disease that had nearly taken his brother's life.

Even as Kutcher pursued his engineering courses, he never lost his desire to act. He carried his dream with him in his wallet; on a small piece of paper Kutcher had written his goal of going to Hollywood to become an actor. But he had real doubts about his abilities. "I was never the star of my high-school plays. My private feeling was, 'You can't even get the lead

The cast of "That '70s Show."

when there are 52 people in your class. How are you possibly going to go to Hollywood?'" Despite his doubts and other obstacles, he decided to quit college and try to become an actor. He packed a bag of gear and started walking to the airport, which was about 30 miles away. He made it about 20 miles but detoured to his mother's house. She drove him back to school, where he finished the semester.

FIRST JOBS

Soon after Kutcher's first attempt to get to Hollywood, a modeling agent approached him and suggested that he enter a statewide modeling competition. "Whoa, do guys even do that?" he wondered. In Homestead men became farmers or factory workers, not models. The only male model he knew of was Fabio, and Kutcher wasn't anything like this muscular model with tanned skin and flowing blond hair. He said he "figured it was a scam," but entered on the urging of a friend.

To his surprise, Kutcher won the Fresh Faces of Iowa modeling contest in 1997 and a trip to the International Modeling and Talent Association's convention in New York. At the convention, a modeling agent noticed him and soon Kutcher had an appointment with talent manager Stephanie Simon. Kutcher immediately impressed Simon. "The second I met him, I just knew," she said. "I knew he was going to be huge. I told him on the spot, 'You're moving to New York' — and he did." Within days, Kutcher began modeling for top designers on runways in New York, Milan, Paris, London, and other parts of the world.

Because there were several other models named Chris at the agency, Kutcher opted to use his middle name, Ashton. Although all his friends and family in Iowa still call him Chris, Ashton Kutcher is the name he uses for the rest of the world.

———— 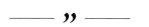 ————

When talent manager Stephanie Simon first met Kutcher, she was immediately impressed. "The second I met him, I just knew," she said. "I knew he was going to be huge. I told him on the spot, 'You're moving to New York' — and he did."

———— ,, ————

Within a year modeling led to acting. Kutcher flew to Los Angeles to test for a television pilot. Though he didn't get that role, he also tested for two others. One part was for an NBC drama called "Wind on Water," and the other was for a Fox sitcom called "That '70s Show." He was offered both roles within hours. He chose to sign for the role of Michael Kelso on "That '70s Show." Kutcher was about to realize his dream.

CAREER HIGHLIGHTS

"That '70s Show"

"That '70s Show" is a sitcom about six teenage friends growing up together in a Wisconsin suburb during the mid-1970s. The series is a nostalgic look at a time when the roles of women, men, and even families were changing in America. The main character of the show is Eric Forman (played by Topher Grace), a likable young man who struggles for independence from the authority of his parents, Red (Kurtwood Smith) and Kitty (Debra Jo Rupp). His family is conservative and solid.

Eric and his group of teenage friends spend most of their time hanging out in Eric's basement talking about their lives. This group includes Donna Pinciotti, Steven Hyde, Fez, Jackie Burkhardt, and Michael Kelso. Donna (Laura Prepon) is Eric's bright, even-tempered girlfriend and next-door neighbor whose parents experiment with every fad and are much more

liberal than the Formans. Hyde (Danny Masterson) lives with Formans, who took him in after his single mother abandoned him. He is a skeptical kid with a dry sense of humor who believes conspiracy theories about big business taking over the world. Fez (Wilmer Valderrama) is a foreign exchange student who is eagerly soaking up American culture. Kelso (Ashton Kutcher) is a good-looking, goofy teenage boy whose gullibility gets him into very funny situations, especially with Jackie (Mila Kunis), his beautiful and spoiled on-again, off-again girlfriend.

The sitcom pokes fun at such 1970s fads as bell bottoms, glam rock music, and polyester clothing, while offering keen insights into the decade's practices and beliefs. Although each episode centers around the comic mishaps of the teenagers, the show also tackles such difficult subjects as open marriages, recreational use of drugs, sex before marriage, and feminism. Kutcher said "The show's writers have nailed what it's like to be a restless Midwestern teen." Since its debut in 1998, the show hit a nerve with the public and critics alike and has become a huge popular success. By now, of course, the group has finished high school and started to grow up, but they still remain best friends.

> "
>
> *"I can't begin to tell you what a pleasure it is working on ['That '70s Show'],"Kutcher said. "I can't get enough of it. It's kind of sick, really."*
>
> "

"That '70s Show" opened up a new world for Kutcher. He dove into his role as Michael Kelso, playing the teenage character as a simple boy who thinks mostly about girls. Kutcher's work on the show confirmed his love of acting. "I can't begin to tell you what a pleasure it is working on that show," he said. "I can't get enough of it. It's kind of sick, really." The character provided a platform for Kutcher's comic talent, but also showed him to be a good-looking, kindhearted guy. Viewers responded to his quirky character and clamored for news about the actor's personal life. After the first season of "That '70s Show," Kutcher had become a teenage heartthrob. *Seventeen* magazine named him "TV's Hottest New Hunk," and *TV Guide, People,* and *US* magazines featured stories about him. While fans swooned over Kutcher, agents vied to cast him in movies.

Becoming a Film Star

Kutcher welcomed the attention and the opportunities for more work. While continuing to work on "That '70s Show," he also began pursuing movie roles. After a few smaller parts, he landed a starring role in the comedy *Dude, Where's My Car?* (2000), which earned him a nomination at the MTV awards in 2001 for Breakthrough Male Performance. In the movie he plays Jesse Richmond, a character very similar to Michael Kelso from "That '70s Show." Jesse and his friend Chester Greenburg, played by Seann William Scott, wake up after a night of partying to discover Jesse's car is missing. Unable to remember what happened to the car, the two try to re-trace their steps from the night before. As they search for the car, they en-

Kutcher and Seann William Scott search for their missing car in Dude, Where's My Car?

counter a number of comic obstacles, including their angry girlfriends, a street gang, a stripper, a cult looking for space aliens, and actual space aliens. Although serious critics ignored the film, viewers enjoyed the wacky, oddball antics of Kutcher and Scott. *Dude, Where's My Car?* became a success at the box office, where it grossed over $46 million.

Kutcher followed this box office hit with a number of other movies, including the western *Texas Rangers* (2000). Set in Texas in 1875, *Texas Rangers* tells the story of a small group of men who band together to battle outlaws in their rugged homeland. Dylan McDermott plays the leader of the Rangers, an unusual mixed group of young adult orphans and older American Civil War veterans, played by actors James Van Der Beek, Ashton Kutcher, Randy Travis, Usher Raymond, and Robert Patrick. *Texas Rangers* tried to capture the essence of old-time western films, but many said it missed the mark. While the story was packed with action, the movie left both viewers and critics wondering why the story and the characters had so little to offer. Kutcher's character in *Texas Rangers* provided comic relief, but wasn't as funny or endearing as Kelso from "That 70's Show."

Kutcher (left), Usher (center), and James Van Der Beek (right)
in a scene from Texas Rangers.

Kutcher and Brittany Murphy in Just Married.

Kutcher had another box office success with the romantic comedy *Just Married* (2003), co-starring Brittany Murphy. The story features Tom and Sarah, a young couple who marry against the wishes of Sarah's family and friends. The movie follows the couple on their honeymoon in Europe as they encounter a series of comic mishaps, from a giant roach crawling in their bed to the attempts of Sarah's ex-boyfriend, sent by her scheming parents, to ruin their marriage. Kutcher portrayed Tom much like a grown-up Kelso, with slapstick comedy and silly facial expressions. The humor in the film was lost on film critics, but viewers pushed it to the top of the box office list. Within weeks of its opening, *Just Married* took in $18 million at the box office and edged *The Lord of the Rings: The Two Towers* from the top spot on the list.

Kutcher played another naïve young man in the romantic comedy *My Boss's Daughter* (2003). Tom (played by Kutcher) is a researcher at a Chicago publishing company. He finds himself overwhelmed as he spends a night trying to look after his boss's house and prized pet owl while a stream of unusual, uninvited houseguests threaten the order of the house and derail his attempts to win over his boss's daughter Lisa (played by Tara Reid). The film is packed with the wild antics of the unusual guests, but the movie didn't win the hearts of either critics or most viewers.

—— " ——

While filming **Just Married,** *Kutcher said he "would work from about eight o'clock in the morning until four in the afternoon on the TV show, and then from four-thirty in the afternoon until four in the morning on the movie, and I would take 15-minute military naps during the day to keep going."*

—— " ——

Kutcher's work in film and on TV earned him a reputation as a hard working actor. While filming *Just Married,* Kutcher said he "would work from about eight o'clock in the morning until four in the afternoon on the TV show, and then from four-thirty in the afternoon until four in the morning on the movie, and I would take 15-minute military naps during the day to keep going." Director of *Texas Rangers* Steve Miner said that Kutcher "just doesn't stop. . . . I wanted to hook up a cable to him to harness some of his energy—it would save on generator costs." Combined, his hard work and his public appeal make Kutcher an actor popular with directors and viewers alike.

Kutcher and Justin Timberlake in a scene from "Punk'd."

"Punk'd"

Kutcher cemented his reputation for hard work by landing his own television series on MTV in 2003. His show, "Punk'd," was a reality-based comedy show in which Kutcher and others played practical jokes on celebrities. In each episode, "Punk'd" cast members used a hidden camera set-up while trying to put television and film stars in awkward and humiliating situations. But these situations seemed so genuine that the celebrities fell for the bait and believed it was real. Kutcher narrated the action from behind the scenes and always revealed the joke to the stars in the end.

In one episode, for example, the "Punk'd" cast members fooled teen actor Hilary Duff (star of the popular television show "Lizzy McGuire") into thinking she was taking a normal driving test. The camera followed Duff's reaction as her instructor offered bad driving advice, leapt from the car to fight with another driver, and eventually ran off, leaving Duff to fend for herself as a man tried to steal the car she was driving. Before any real damage was done, Kutcher appeared, much to Duff's relief. In another episode, Justin Timberlake was devastated when he found fake IRS (Internal Revenue Service) agents confiscating his house, possessions, and pets. A few of the other stars who have been "punk'd" include Kelly Osbourne, daughter of the rock star Ozzie Osbourne, Frankie Muniz, star of

"Malcolm in the Middle," singers Usher, Pink, and Mandy Moore, rappers Missy Elliott and OutKast, and Kutcher's costar from "That '70s Show," Wilmer Valderrama.

"Punk'd" aired for two seasons on MTV. Then in December 2003, Kutcher announced that he was ending the show. "We have had an incredible time doing the show," he announced, "and have decided to stick with the old adage of 'leave em wanting more.'" Lois Curren, an MTV executive in charge of series development, said that "Today is a sad day for MTV, but probably a happy day for Hollywood. Celebrities can rest a little easier knowing that the Punkings have ceased." Beyonce Knowles was the final victim, when she appeared at a charity Christmas event for young orphans. She tried to place a star on top of the Christmas tree, the tree fell on top of the presents and crushed them, and Beyonce was convinced that she had ruined it for the young orphans, who of course were already in on the joke. Still, many wondered if perhaps the announcement was itself a joke and if Kutcher planned to resume the show later.

In December 2003, Kutcher announced that he was ending "Punk'd." "We have had an incredible time doing the show," he announced, "and have decided to stick with the old adage of 'leave em wanting more.'"

A Bright Future

Along with his work on "That 70's Show," Kutcher continues to act in and produce movies. His most recent project is the production of and starring role in *The Butterfly Effect* (2004). The movie is based on a scientific argument called the "butterfly effect," which explores how seemingly small changes in one part of the world might have a huge impact on another. The phrase refers to an idea based on chaos theory of cause and effect, that a butterfly flapping its wings in one part of the world could set off climactic changes that would result in a tsunami somewhere else. In this sci-fi thriller, Kutcher plays a tormented young man who, while attempting to deal with hurtful childhood memories, discovers how to travel back in time. As he alters his own history, he discovers that he has also changed his future. This more serious and dramatic role was a big shift for Kutcher, and he took his part in the film very seriously. "I don't think people think I can handle a dramatic movie. So I want to be good. No, I want to be great," Kutcher said. Unfortunately, most critics and even his fans faulted

Kutcher stars as Evan in the thriller The Butterfly Effect.

the movie as pretentious and muddled and disparaged his acting as inept, and it was a flop at the box office.

Still, Kutcher's future looks very promising. He is in the center of the public eye, being voted "Hottest Bachelor" by *People* magazine readers in 2003, and he has many fans who enjoy his more light-hearted TV shows and movies. About his life, Kutcher notes that "I don't believe good things come to those who wait. I believe that good things come to those who want something so bad, they can't wait."

HOME AND FAMILY

Kutcher moved to Los Angeles when he began working on "That '70s Show" in 1998. Although he misses his family, he often returns to visit them in Iowa. His twin brother works at an insurance company and his sister teaches art at an elementary school.

Kutcher has never married, but he has had a series of high profile romances since entering show business. He has also been romantically linked with his co-stars on several projects, including Brittany Murphy from *Just Married* and Amy Smart from *The Butterfly Effect*. But it is his relationship with the actress Demi Moore that has created the biggest media stir. Moore was the highest-paid female actor in Hollywood when she dropped her high-profile life in 1998 to raise her three children in Idaho. Reports that Kutcher and Moore were dating coincided with his rapid rise to fame and her return to movies after a five-year break. The 15-year age difference between Kutcher and Moore has inspired much curiosity and gossip about the relationship. In Hollywood, it is not unusual for women to date older men, but it is very unusual for men to date older women. Some skeptics wonder whether Kutcher and Moore's romance is real or only a publicity stunt to fuel their careers. Only time will tell.

> *About his life, Kutcher notes that "I don't believe good things come to those who wait. I believe that good things come to those who want something so bad, they can't wait."*

MEMORABLE EXPERIENCES

In 2003 Kutcher came face to face with his own fame. While driving by the 20th Century Fox lot, he and his friends noticed his face on a billboard advertising the movie *Just Married*. They pulled over to take a picture. "So I'm standing there like, 'This is ridiculous. I've made it,'" Kutcher said. "And this girl pulls up and looks at the billboard, looks at me, and starts laugh-

———— **"** ————

To spur him to do more with his life, Kutcher taped a piece of paper to his phone on which he wrote "Dream Bigger."
"So, if you see a guy standing in front of his own movie poster," Kutcher jokes, "that's me, trying to think of a dream that's bigger than my billboard."

———— **"** ————

ing hysterically. Because I was standing there looking at my own billboard thinking, 'Wow.'" Kutcher added, "It's the most bizarre thing in the world when your dreams become reality." To spur him to do more with his life, Kutcher taped a piece of paper to his phone on which he wrote "Dream Bigger." "So, if you see a guy standing in front of his own movie poster," Kutcher jokes, "that's me, trying to think of a dream that's bigger than my billboard."

HOBBIES AND OTHER INTERESTS

Kutcher loves collecting hats, including the trucker hats he wore on his MTV show "Punk'd." He is a good cook himself, but ranks his mom's enchiladas as his favorite food. Kutcher doesn't "think you can live a good life without a dog," and he owns a black lab named Willy Wonka and a golden retriever named Mr. Bojangles. An excellent carpenter, he built his own earthquake-proof deck and is redecorating his home.

Despite his stardom, Kutcher hasn't forgotten his commitment to help his brother and others with diseases. He's recorded public announcements for and donated money to health-related charities.

SELECTED CREDITS

Television Series

"That '70s Show," 1998-
"Punk'd," 2003 (co-creator, executive producer, and host)

Movies

Coming Soon, 1999
Down to You, 2000
Reindeer Games, 2000
Dude, Where's My Car? 2000
Texas Rangers, 2001

Just Married, 2003
My Boss's Daughter, 2003 (co-producer and actor)
Cheaper by the Dozen, 2003
The Butterfly Effect, 2004 (co-producer and actor)

HONORS AND AWARDS

Teen Choice Awards: 2003 (four awards), Best TV Actor in a Comedy, for "That '70s Show"; Reality/Variety TV Host and Reality Hunk, for "Punk'd"; Male Hottie

FURTHER READING

Books

Contemporary Theatre, Film and Television, Vol. 39, 2002
Krulik, Nancy. *Second to None: Superstars on the Rise*, 2000

Periodicals

Cosmopolitan, Feb. 2001, p.174; Apr. 2003, p.138
Des Moines Register, Jan. 24, 1999, p.E1; Feb. 3, 2001, p.1; July 4, 2003, p.1 (Iowa Life section)
GQ, Mar. 2000, p.341
InStyle, Feb. 2003, p.121
Interview, Mar. 2000, p.70
Los Angeles Times, June 20, 1998 p.F1; Aug. 10, 2003, p.E1
Louisville (Ky.) Courier-Journal, July 25, 2003, p.C1
New York Post, Mar. 17, 2003, p.79
People, Nov. 2, 1998, p.75; June 16, 2003, p.108; June 30, 2003, p.60
Premiere, Aug. 2000, p.74
Rolling Stone, May 29, 2003, p.44
Seventeen, Feb. 2003, p. 84
Teen, Sep. 2000, p.64
Teen People, July 30, 2003, p.14
USA Today, Dec. 11, 1998, p.E12
Washington Post, Feb. 6, 2000

Online Articles

http://www.eonline.com/Features/Features/Kutcher/
(*Eonline.com*, "How That Kutcher Dude Went from a Nobody to A-List Gossip Bait in No Time Flat," June 27, 2003)

http://abcnews.go.com/sections/Entertainment/SciTech/ashton_kutcher_
040123-1.html (ABC News, "Dude, Where's My Joke? Kutcher Yearns to
Be Taken Seriously," Jan. 23, 2004)

Online Databases

Biography Resource Center Online, 2004, article from *Contemporary Theatre,
Film and Television*, 2002

ADDRESS

Ashton Kutcher
Endeavor Talent Agency
9701 Wilshire Blvd., 10th Floor
Beverly Hills, CA 90212

WORLD WIDE WEB SITES

http://www.that70sshow.com
http://www.mtv.com
http://www.butterflyeffectmovie.com

John Mayer 1977-

American Singer and Songwriter
Creator of the Hit CDs *Room for Squares* and
Heavier Things

BIRTH

John Mayer was born on October 16, 1977, in Bridgeport,
Connecticut. His father, Richard Mayer, was a high school
principal. His mother, Margaret Mayer, was a middle school
English teacher. They have lived in the same house since 1984.
John has an older brother, Carl, and a younger brother, Ben.

YOUTH

Mayer grew up in Fairfield, Connecticut. According to his mother, Mayer was always "a peaceable kid. He would not demand a lot of attention. He would go off and do things by himself." Mayer participated in middle school and high school theater until he turned his attention to music.

Mayer has been exposed to music all his life. His father would often play jazz standards and show tunes on the piano at home. He also played the piano at the weekly Rotary Club meetings. "Growing up in Connecticut," Mayer recalled, "there was a piano in the house from the time I was born, and I just gravitated toward it." He would sit at the piano and create sounds out of nothing. He didn't really want to learn how to play the piano; he just wanted to play it.

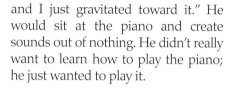

> *"Growing up in Connecticut," Mayer recalled, "there was a piano in the house from the time I was born, and I just gravitated toward it." He would sit at the piano and create sounds out of nothing. He didn't really want to learn how to play the piano; he just wanted to play it.*

When he was 13 years old, Mayer got his first guitar. The first night he had the guitar, he tried to figure out how to play it by himself, and it didn't take long for him to figure out chords. He had the guitar for two weeks before he took lessons. After several months of guitar lessons, his parents stopped his lessons because he was not learning to read music.

In 1990, Mayer's neighbor gave him a tape of Stevie Ray Vaughan, a bluesy rock guitarist. When he listened to it, he thought, "What is this and where is the rest of it?" He became obsessed with Vaughan and such other rock guitarists as Jimi Hendrix, Buddy Guy, and Robert Cray. Soon, Mayer was spending all his free time playing guitar. Consequently, his grades suffered. Mayer asked his parents more than once to let him drop out of high school; he didn't think school was necessary since he was going to be a famous guitarist. His parents became concerned and sent him to two different therapists to try to convince him to stop playing guitar.

When Mayer was just 15 years old, he started playing guitar in clubs around the area. In the early 1990s, he and a high school friend, Joe Beleznay, played in a band called Villanova Junction. The band did not last long, but Mayer and Beleznay continued to work together on their music. The two went their separate ways when Mayer left for college.

When he was young, Mayer vowed that he would not drink alcohol or take drugs. "I really did say growing up that I won't drink and do drugs," he swears. "I wanted to shape my life toward making records." And he has kept that vow throughout his success.

EDUCATION

In 1995, Mayer graduated from Fairfield High School, home of the Fairfield Mustangs. He spent the next two years working at a gas station just a quarter of a mile from his parents' house. He continued to play his music at local clubs, determined to pursue a career in music. Eventually, however, he realized that he needed to do something more if he wanted to succeed in music. He remembers thinking, "OK. It's not going to happen here. It's not going to happen in Connecticut. It's not going to happen living at home." That's when he decided to enroll at the prestigious Berklee College of Music in Boston, Massachusetts. Such famous musical performers as Quincy Jones, Bruce Hornsby, and Natalie Maines of the Dixie Chicks had also studied at Berklee.

After less than one year at Berklee, Mayer decided that he had had enough. He felt that the school emphasized technical expertise rather than creativity. He soon started to skip classes and then eventually dropped out. "I went to Berklee by default," Mayer said. "I really had an interest in songwriting, and I eventually dropped out to write songs. . . . I have been an observationalist all my life, and I wanted to write songs in a way they hadn't been written before. I want to be the guy that people say hit the nail on the head with my lyrics, and I want to tell things from my perspective, not be a third-person storyteller. But I felt that I hadn't hit my mark yet."

CAREER HIGHLIGHTS

Starting Off Small

Mayer left Berklee with one of his classmates, Clay Cook, and headed to Atlanta, Georgia, to try to start a music career. (Cook later co-wrote three songs on Mayer's *Room for Squares* CD.) "The concept was to move to

someplace completely new and start from scratch," Mayer said. "I wanted the plane to touch down somewhere that I knew nothing of before going there. Atlanta was becoming a really cool place for singer-songwriters. So it became this mission for me to move down and just start playing."

When Mayer first arrived in Atlanta, he panicked. He had just dropped out of college with failing grades, and he had an outstanding bill from Berklee for supposedly drawing on his dormitory room wall. He found a day job at a videotape duplication factory. At night, he wrote songs and played his guitar at local coffee houses and clubs. He performed regularly at Eddie's Attic in Decatur, a popular hang-out for aspiring young musicians. Audiences loved him, and he soon developed a following. Mayer said, "People would go, 'You have a CD?' And I'd go, 'No,' and they'd put their $20 bill back in their pocket. That'll make you make a CD really fast."

Mayer took his music to several major record companies, hoping to secure a record contract. He was turned down time after time by these companies, however, because his musical style was so different from the music that was popular at the time. Mayer recalls, "I was so discouraged. It was so counterproductive that someone could sit in front of me and say, 'The direction's just going into like, really heavy metal and boy bands, and it's the flavor of the day right now.' I was very frustrated by that—that even the people who take risks, take calculated risks that are so calculated that they're not [risks]." Even though the record companies were not interested in his music, his popularity was growing among local fans. So in 1999, Mayer put his songs on a CD and released it himself. He titled the CD *Inside Wants Out* and spent the next two years touring the United States to promote it.

> *Record companies turned Mayer down repeatedly because his musical style was so different from the music that was popular at the time. "I was so discouraged," Mayer recalls. "It was so counterproductive that someone could sit in front of me and say, 'The direction's just going into like, really heavy metal and boy bands, and it's the flavor of the day right now.' I was very frustrated by that."*

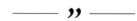

Defining Mayer's Music Appeal

Mayer is often compared to Dave Matthews of the Dave Matthews Band. He has also been compared to Sting, Ben Folds, and other artists. But Mayer has his own, individual style. When he first started to play the guitar, he played mostly blues. Over time, his musical style has changed. When asked to classify it, Mayer said, "It's definitely pop music with some jazz influence." Music critic Doug Hamilton from the *Atlanta Journal-Constitution* described Mayer's music as a "sophisticated, accessible folk-rock sound dominated by striking acoustic guitar playing, video-ready looks, and a sizeable grass-roots following born in clubs across the South." And the reviewer from *Rolling Stone* described his sound as "curving, melodically rich tunes that weave folk, blues, rock, and wisps of jazz."

Mayer's music appeals to people of all ages with all different musical tastes. He said, "I've met 60-year-old people at my shows, and I've signed autographs for 6 year-old girls." His goal is to make music that appeals to as many people as possible. "If I'm making music that people come to, I don't

*Mayer poses for a photo backstage with just a small portion
of the equipment that's required on tour.*

care who comes," Mayer said. "I don't care if they're 15 years old; I don't
care if they're embryos. I'm not aiming it towards anybody; I'm aiming it towards everybody." That accessible and modest quality is part of his appeal.
"A big part of the singer-songwriter's charm," according to the *Boston Globe*,
"is the unassuming attitude that characterizes both him and his music."

Rising to Stardom

In March 2000, Mayer traveled to Austin, Texas, to perform at the annual
South by Southwest conference. This conference, known for discovering
alternative rock artists, is where he received his first big break. Many of the
major record companies were there and saw how the crowds reacted to his
music. By the end of the conference, representatives from several record
companies had given Mayer their business cards. He soon signed a contract with Aware Records, a subsidiary of Columbia Records.

In August 2000, Mayer traveled to the Atlantis Music Conference. The pur-
pose of the Conference is to focus the national and international music industry and related press on Atlanta's growing, talented, and diverse music
scene at a national level. As part of Atlantis, Mayer was presented an

award for Favorite Songwriter from ASCAP (American Society of Composers, Authors, and Publishers).

Mayer was still relatively unknown at the time, but he quickly gained exposure by word of mouth. According to the president of Aware Records, "If he plays for ten people, they'll all buy his CD and tell their friends." Mayer believes that allowing people to download music via the Internet also helped to boost his popularity. He has even called it his "saving grace." He believes that downloading music should be a right. He told the Internet site Yahoo! that "people don't have to be assaulted by this giant wheel of color and someone's image presentation; it's just a song and whether you like it or not. . . . And I think that people, in the beginning, were introduced to my music that way."

Room for Squares

With the support of his new record company, Mayer started work on his second CD, *Room for Squares*. The music on *Room for Squares* is much different from that on *Inside Wants Out*. There is far less blues influence on this second CD, and most of the songs were recorded with a full band.

When asked how he came up with the title for his CD, Mayer replied, "I'm a jazz fan and I was flipping through a Blue Note Records coffee

When asked how he came up with the title for his CD, Mayer replied, "I'm a jazz fan and I was flipping through a Blue Note Records coffee table book and saw [Hank] Mobley's album [No Room for Squares]. *There was something about the words. I'm kind of a word guy, and it just looked great."*

table book and saw [Hank] Mobley's album [*No Room for Squares*]. There was something about the words. I'm kind of a word guy, and it just looked great." It's not surprising that he's a word guy. Mayer said that he has been in love with words since he was a child. "My mother is an English teacher," he said. "I always wanted to impress her. I still travel with a dictionary and look up a word every day."

By the time Mayer released *Room for Squares* in September 2001, he was becoming better known. Radio stations of all types started to play songs from the CD, including "No Such Thing" and "Your Body Is a Wonderland." In fact, "No Such Thing" was one of the most played songs all over the country—in Chicago, Illinois; Boston, Massachusetts; Portland,

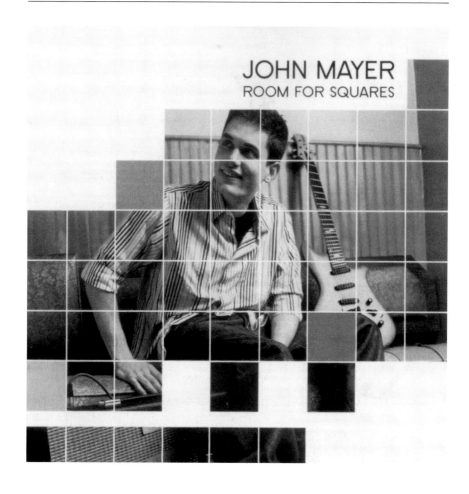

Oregon; Baltimore, Maryland; and Memphis, Tennessee. And his music was being played on stations with a variety of formats: modern adult contemporary, modern rock, and top 40 stations were all playing his song.

Soon, music critics were touting this new work. *Rolling Stone* gave *Room for Squares* four stars in its December 2001 review of the CD. In February 2002, Mayer was named one of the "10 Artists to Watch" on the *Rolling Stone* web site. As his music continued to receive more airplay, his record sales grew. By July 2002, *Room for Squares* was certified platinum (one million copies sold). At one point when Mayer was struggling at Berklee, his father had sent him a check for $250. He had attached a note that read, "John, remember me when you go platinum." Mayer kept that note. When he received his first platinum record plaque, he mounted his father's note inside the frame and gave it to his father. *Room for Squares* remained in the Top 100 after 80 straight weeks and reached triple platinum status by May 2003.

As Mayer's popularity continued to grow, he began to get more attention from the music industry. In August 2002, he was nominated for Best New Artist in the MTV Video Music Awards. In February 2003, he earned a nomination for Best New Artist at the Grammy Awards. Although he did not win that award, he did win the 2003 Grammy Award for Best Male Pop Vocal Performance for "Your Body is a Wonderland," beating Elton John, Sting, and James Taylor. In August 2003, "Your Body is a Wonderland" was nominated for Best Male Video at the MTV Video Music Awards. In October 2003, Mayer won the Artist of the Year — Adult Contemporary Radio at the Radio Music Awards. Also in October 2003, he was nominated for Favorite Pop/Rock Male Artist at the American Music Awards.

At one point when Mayer was struggling at Berklee, his father had sent him a check for $250. He had attached a note that read, "John, remember me when you go platinum." Mayer kept that note. When he received his first platinum record plaque for **Room for Squares,** *he mounted his father's note inside the frame and gave it to his father.*

Any Given Thursday

In February 2003, Mayer released a live album titled *Any Given Thursday.* The two-disc set is a recording of a concert he performed on September 12, 2002, in Birmingham, Alabama. This was one of the last concerts on Mayer's summer 2002 tour. A DVD of the concert was released at the same time. Most of the songs performed during that concert are from the *Room for Squares* CD. By August 2003, *Any Given Thursday* was certified platinum.

Perhaps the CD set achieved such quick success because fans wanted to see and hear more of Mayer's live music. Mayer had gained most of his early exposure through his relentless touring, and these stage performances were widely praised by music critics. As he continued to gain recognition, his shows started to sell out, sometimes to crowds as large as 10,000 people. He even allows his fans to record most of his live shows, as long as the recordings are for personal use or trading only. The recordings cannot be sold or commercialized in any way. Mayer clearly enjoys playing his music live, and he appreciates his audiences at his live shows. The *Richmond Times Dispatch* said that "only those who have seen him live

147

would know the kid is a terrific guitarist, capable of noodling blues riffs that would make his idol, Stevie Ray Vaughan, proud."

Heavier Things

Soon Mayer went to work on *Heavier Things*, his third album on a major record label. Mayer felt that he was somewhat under pressure when he was making this CD. "There was pressure artistically for me to make another good record, a better record in some respects," he said at the time. "But I never looked at a platinum plaque on my wall and went, 'Oh, how do I get another one of these?'"

The subjects of the songs on *Heavier Things* are more serious than those on *Room for Squares*. Mayer considered naming this album *Home Life*, the title of one song on the CD, because of his strong domestic leanings. Throughout his music, he expresses the desire to find stability, true love, and home. "Bigger Than My Body," the first single, is a song about "not being where you want to get in your life," Mayer said. "It's going to sound silly when people first hear it." He though that people would wonder why he was singing about making it someday when he had already made it. "Whether or not you win a Grammy, it doesn't really modify the plan," Mayer continued. "'Bigger Than My Body' is about the feeling you get when you want to be more and you can't." Mayer said that he loves *Room for Squares*, but *Heavier Things* has more emotional weight to it.

> "[Heavier Things *is*] superior to Squares. *The songs are more focused, the musical backdrops are more varied and informed more by '60s soul and modern R&B, the production is lusher and thicker. And Mayer, in general, sounds more mature and comfortable within his music."* — Fort Worth Star Telegram

By the time Mayer released *Heavier Things,* his fans were eagerly waiting. In September 2003, MTV's web site gave fans the opportunity to preview *Heavier Things* when it made the album available for streaming (listening to it online). There were 1.3 million tracks requested, more than any other title featured. When the CD was finally released on September 9, 2003, it debuted at No. 1 on the music charts and sold over 315,000 copies in the U.S. during its first week. By October 2003, the album was certified platinum. Fans were buying the CD, and critics began to rave about it, too. For

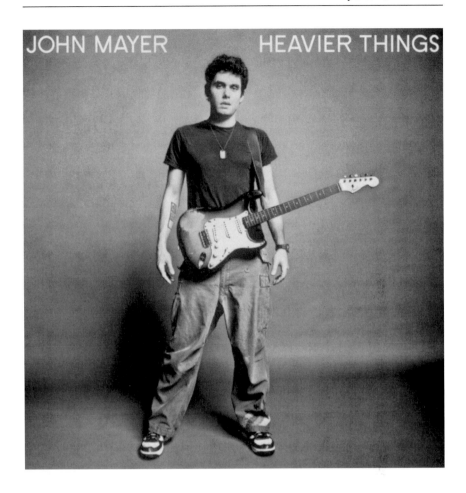

example, the *Fort Worth Star Telegram* said that *Heavier Things* is "superior to *Squares*. The songs are more focused, the musical backdrops are more varied and informed more by '60s soul and modern R&B, the production is lusher and thicker. And Mayer, in general, sounds more mature and comfortable within his music."

Living with Fame

Mayer's popularity led to appearances on several television shows, including "Late Night with Conan O'Brien," "The Tonight Show with Jay Leno," "Saturday Night Live," "Prime Time," "Last Call with Carson Daly," "The Late, Late Show with Craig Kilborn," and "Austin City Limits." In addition, his song "Not Myself," appears on the original motion picture soundtrack for the 2003 movie, *How to Deal*.

But for Mayer, all this attention was not important. "I don't want to be a famous person, he told *Rolling Stone,* "I want to be a famous musician."
Although he enjoys some of the benefits of being a celebrity, he also has
had to face the challenges of being so widely recognized. Because he is
young, attractive, and single, he is often asked about his love life. Many of
the words to his songs are so sincere, leading Mayer to be labeled a "sensitive guy." When *Teen People* magazine compiled a list of the Hottest
Entertainers Under 25 in 2003, Mayer was on the list as the "Hottest
Sensitive Guy." *YM* magazine also named him one of the "20 Hottest
Guys" in its August 2003 issue.

One of Mayer's biggest and most famous fans is singer Elton John. John has publicly praised Mayer's music and even interviewed him for the April 2002 issue of *Interview* magazine. Mayer is also a fan of Elton John. In January 2001, Mayer performed with several other musical artists in a benefit to pay tribute to him. The benefit raised money for music education. Mayer was the only performer to actually sing with John that night. The two sang John's first No. 1 single, "Sacrifice." Mayer and John are friends, and John will occasionally give Mayer advice.

Mayer credits singer Glenn Phillips, lead singer for Toad the Wet Sprocket, with teaching him how to handle fame and deal with fans. Mayer said, "I was able to see how he made himself available to people and fans. If I was left to my own devices, I probably would have imagined that I was going to be less accessible, because that's just the way it had to be." But Phillips gave him some valuable advice. According to Mayer, "Glenn was like, 'Here's how you are to people: you look them in the eye, you thank them, and it's OK to give them the same compassion and love that you would give to someone that you're meeting at a family get-together.'"

> *Mayer credits singer Glenn Phillips, lead singer for Toad the Wet Sprocket, for teaching him how to handle fame and deal with fans. Phillips gave him some valuable advice. According to Mayer, "Glenn was like, 'Here's how you are to people: you look them in the eye, you thank them, and it's OK to give them the same compassion and love that you would give to someone that you're meeting at a family get-together.'"*

HOME AND FAMILY

Mayer currently lives in a duplex in Manhattan in New York City. His duplex overlooks the Empire State Building and includes a recording studio on the second floor. This is where he recorded most of the songs for *Heavier Things*.

Mayer has never been married but would very much like to settle down some day. He says he has not yet found his soul mate, but he knows that he will someday. According to Mayer, "That is somebody who is confident enough to feel love at a moment when love is not being given. A lot of times, I feel like I'm on the road to support a family I don't even have yet. I don't have to tour as much as I do, but I want to for that future family."

When asked if it would be hard to have a serious relationship when he's on tour all the time, he said, "I would give this all up right now for a wife if it meant that if I didn't give it all up I'd never find one. Money? It's nothing until it means taking care of a wife and kids. I will gladly be former one-time successful rock musician John Mayer who pitches the first ball at Little League games."

MAJOR INFLUENCES

According to Mayer, "When I was a kid, I was influenced by whoever was on the radio — Michael Jackson and the Police and bands like that. Until I picked up a tape of Stevie Ray Vaughan's music. . . . My life was different once I heard that. I didn't know what that was, but I wanted to do it." Mayer said that the first moment he became interested in playing music was right after he heard Vaughan. "I got lost in the primal roots and the music spoke to me," he said. And even though his later music is more pop than blues, he still considers Vaughan his idol. Every time he holds a guitar, he still holds it like Vaughan. He said, "Anyone who has an idol is still going to reference themselves against the silhouette of their idol."

Mayer also lists Eric Clapton, Bonnie Raitt, Elton John, Ben Folds Five, Martin Sexton, and Freedy Johnston among his musical influences. Mayer said that he often watches an Eric Clapton concert DVD before his own performances so that he can remember how to "hold the stage without letting the stage crush him."

"When I was a kid, I was influenced by whoever was on the radio — Michael Jackson and the Police and bands like that. Until I picked up a tape of Stevie Ray Vaughan's music. . . . My life was different once I heard that. I didn't know what that was, but I wanted to do it."

HOBBIES AND OTHER INTERESTS

Mayer has said that he has no hobbies or interests outside of music. However, while on the road, he and his bandmates play video games on an XBox on the band's tour bus. In fact, they enjoy playing the sniper video game *Halo* so much that they wear fake Army dog tags with the names of their *Halo* aliases.

RECORDINGS

Inside Wants Out, 1999, re-released 2002
Room for Squares, 2001
Any Given Thursday, 2003
Heavier Things, 2003

HONORS AND AWARDS

Grammy Award (National Academy of Recording Arts and Sciences):
    2003, Best Male Pop Vocal Performance, for "Your Body is a Wonderland"
Radio Music Award: 2003, Artist of the Year — Adult Contemporary Radio

FURTHER READING

Periodicals

Atlanta Journal-Constitution, May 6, 2001, p.C6
Boston Globe, Feb. 22, 2002, p.D16
Cleveland Plain Dealer, July 24, 2002, p.E1; Aug. 8. 2003, p.4
Fort Worth Star-Telegram, Sep. 19, 2003, p.S25
Guitar Player, Feb. 2004, p.64
Guitar World Acoustic, Dec. 2003, p.28
Interview, Apr. 2002, p.114
Portland (Me.) Press Herald, Nov. 21, 2002, p.D3
Richmond (Va.) Times Dispatch, Feb. 20, 2003, p.D16
San Diego Union-Tribune, Aug. 15, 2002, Night & Day section, p.4
Tampa Tribune, Nov. 5, 2002, p.2
Teen People, June 1, 2002, p.99
YM, Aug. 2003, p.102

ADDRESS

John Mayer
Columbia Records
550 Madison Avenue
New York, NY 10022

WORLD WIDE WEB SITES

http://www.johnmayer.com
http://www.mtv.com/bands/az/mayer_john/artist.jhtml
http://www.vh1.com/artists/az/mayer_john/bio.jhtml

Raven 1985-
American Actress and Singer
Star of "That's So Raven" and *The Cheetah Girls*

BIRTH

Raven-Symone Christina Pearman, known as Raven to her
many fans, was born on December 10, 1985, in Atlanta, Georgia. Her parents are Lydia Gaulden Pearman and Christopher
Barnard Pearman. According to her parents, Raven was named
for the first bird that Noah released from the Ark. "When the
rain had subsided, Noah released the raven first, not the dove,"
her father says. "The raven is very, very intelligent. And to us,
she was this beautiful black bird . . . her spirit was high and
free."

When Raven was born, Lydia was a computer systems analyst and Christopher was a musician. Now, they're both involved in managing Raven's career, with Christopher writing music and producing for his talented daughter. Raven also has a younger brother named Blaize.

CAREER HIGHLIGHTS

Raven got started in show business as a baby. When she was just 16 months old, she became a baby model for an Atlanta department store and was soon appearing in television commercials for nationally known products like Ritz Crackers, Cheerios, and Cool Whip.

Raven credits Cosby with teaching her some important things about show business. "Stay professional and always stay sweet," he told her. "I haven't been the kid on the set that throws tantrums, even today," she says now. "That advice still works. Thanks, Mr. Cosby."

"The Cosby Show"

According to her parents, Raven was a very bright young toddler. "She was saying her ABCs and the Pledge of Allegiance when she was two," says her dad. One day, while watching "The Cosby Show," she announced, "I can do what Rudy can do." She was talking about the actress Keshia Knight Pullman, who played Bill Cosby's youngest daughter on "The Cosby Show," one of the most popular comedies ever on television. The Pearmans decided to give Raven a chance. They took her to New York, where the Cosby show was filmed, and her parents signed her with the prestigious Ford modeling agency. That led to other contacts, which led to an audition for a TV movie, "Ghost Dad." She didn't get the part, but the show's producers were impressed with her and they thought Cosby would be, too. (For more information on Cosby, see *Biography Today*, Jan. 1992.)

Raven met and talked to Bill Cosby, and he loved her. He added a part to the show for her, and she was on her way. From 1989 to 1992, she played the role of Olivia, the stepdaughter of Denise, played by Lisa Bonet. (At this point, while working on "The Cosby Show," she used the name Raven-Symone as her professional name.) Raven soon became a favorite with viewers all over the country. Her family moved to New York, where her dad took her to work and spent every day on the set.

Raven with Bill Cosby on the set of the TV series "The Cosby Show."

Her father also worked with Raven on her lines. He remembers that he would read the scripts to her as if they were a story. Raven was always a quick learner, and she loved it. Cosby was amazed. "She is professional in every way," he said in an interview in 1990. "Raven comes to the studio on time, knows her lines, and is ready to work." She doesn't remember too much about the show, but does recall that she loved the cast, and Cosby especially. She credits him with teaching her some important things about show business. "Stay professional and always stay sweet," he told her. "I haven't been the kid on the set that throws tantrums, even today," she says now. "That advice still works. Thanks, Mr. Cosby."

Early Projects

Raven's first acting job after "Cosby" was in the made for TV movie *Queen*, which broadcast in 1993. It was based on the last work of the African-American author Alex Haley, who wrote *Roots*. (For more information on Haley, see *Biography Today*, April 1992.) *Queen* was Haley's tribute to his own grandmother, who had been born a slave in the South in the 19th century. Raven played Queen as a five year old.

> *Raven has some funny memories about making* **Dr. Doolittle** *with Eddie Murphy. "He does things to see how well you can not laugh," she says. "When the camera's rolling and the scene is supposed to be over, he keeps going and ad-libbing, and it's really hard to keep a straight face."*

Raven next moved on to the world of music. Her parents knew she loved to sing, and they arranged a contract for her with MCA Records. Her first album, titled *Here's to New Dreams*, was recorded when she was five and released three years later, in 1993. She was the youngest star ever to sign a contract with MCA. Her dad co-wrote three of the songs, including the title track, "Here's to New Dreams." Raven made other musical appearances at the time, including a Broadway debut singing with the Boys' Choir of Harlem in 1993.

The same year her first record came out, Raven joined the cast of another TV hit, "Hangin' with Mr. Cooper." The show, which starred Mark Curry, featured Raven as Cooper's niece Nicole, a sassy, smart little girl who steals her uncle's heart. She was delighted with the role. "I love this show," she said in 1993. "It's great working with Mark. He's real, real tall and real, real funny." For Raven, the character of Nicole was very different from Olivia. "For one, I'm a lot older here. Olivia was a lot younger. Olivia has grown into Nicole. I'm in a new city and trying to learn new things." Raven played the role for four years, from 1993 to 1997, and when the show ended, she went back to music.

Raven's second album, *Undeniable*, featured a new single, "With a Child's Heart," that was written by Stevie Wonder. Wonder wrote another song for

Raven and Eddie Murphy in a scene from Dr. Doolittle 2.

the album, and Raven also got to spend time with the great musician in the studio. "He was wonderful!" she claimed. "I got to work with him for three days." *Undeniable* also featured a song she had written, "Best Friend," and several written by her father and the record's producer. To promote the record and her singing career, Raven toured with 'N Sync, one of the most popular boy bands of the era. She loved performing and touring, but always kept her hand in acting, too.

Raven made a brief appearance in *The Little Rascals*, a 1994 film version of the beloved TV classic. She enjoyed it very much, and her parents looked for other good roles. Raven made several guest appearances on TV, performing in shows like "A Different World," "The Fresh Prince of Bel-Air," and "Sesame Street."

More Recent Projects

In 1998, Raven appeared in *Dr. Doolittle*, which starred Eddie Murphy (see *Biography Today Performing Artists*, Vol. 2). The movie followed the misadventures of Murphy as Dr. Doolittle, a famous vet who can talk to animals—and they talk back. Raven played Murphy's oldest daughter, Charisse, and has some funny memories about making the movie. "He does things to see how well you can not laugh," she says. "When the camera's rolling and the scene is supposed to be over, he keeps going and ad-libbing, and it's really hard to keep a straight face."

Raven's next film was a made-for-TV movie titled *Zenon: Girl of the 21st Century*, which first aired on the Disney Channel in 1999. Raven played Nebula, the best friend of Zenon, played by Kirsten Storms. The movie is based on the children's book by Marilyn Salder and Roger Bollen, which also became a comic strip. The movie is set in the year 2049 and features the exploits of Zenon as she spends some time on Earth unraveling the clues to a mystery involving the space station she calls home.

> *"I thought she looked just like me!" Raven said about her animated character Monique on "Kim Possible." "The animators watch you while you're talking to see your facial expressions and the way you move your hands while you talk, and they try to copy that for the cartoon characters."*

In 2001, Raven returned to the big screen again in *Dr. Doolittle 2*, a sequel to the earlier movie. Once again, she played Eddie Murphy's daughter, and once again the set was filled with all kinds of rambunctious animals. "I love the monkey, Crystal, who I held on my shoulders," Raven recalled. "Crystal's really sweet, very friendly, and doesn't bite." Not all the animals were so easy to get along with. "Once, when I was holding the chameleon, he wouldn't let go of my hand. I was wearing lace and he kept sticking to it—they had to pull him off."

"Kim Possible"

In 2002, Raven appeared as the voice of Monique on the hit cartoon "Kim Possible," which appears on the Disney Channel. The show features the exploits of teenager Kim, who seems like a normal kid, but who really possesses secret powers. Raven says it's fun to play her friend Monique "because I just get to go crazy on her voice. I can do all types of ups and downs and not have to worry about how my face is coming off on screen." When she first saw her animated character on the show, she was amazed. "I thought she looked just like me!" she recalls. "The animators watch you while you're talking to see your facial expressions and the way you move your hands while you talk, and they try to copy that for the cartoon characters."

A scene from "Kim Possible."

Big Breakout: "That's So Raven"

Raven's big breakout role came in 2003, when she starred in a new Disney Channel hit, "That's So Raven." The show debuted in January 2003, and soon it was one of the most popular on the network. She plays Raven Baxter, a teenager who's psychic—but with a twist. She can see into the future, but she doesn't see everything in quite the right way. "It's all about a girl who has psychic visions," Raven explains. "However, as the visions are always incomplete, she has to figure out exactly what they mean. This often lands her and her friends in hot water." The show is hilarious, with Raven and her two best friends, Eddie (Orlando Brown) and Chelsea (Anneliese van der Pol), trying to avoid the disaster that always seems to come their way as they try to figure out the future. Raven has been praised for her slapstick, physical humor, which came easily. "In real life, I just be fallin' all over the place unintentionally, so I just told them to put my clumsiness on the screen," she says.

"We have such a laugh on the set," she says. "There's a lot of physical comedy in the show, especially dressing up in strange and weird costumes. It's a real blast." Some commentators have compared her comedic talents to those of TV icon Lucille Ball. Raven graciously accepts the compliment, saying that she's loved watching "I Love Lucy" reruns for years. Disney's delighted with her success, too. In fact, the original title for the show was

Raven with the cast from her hit Disney show "That's So Raven."

"Absolutely Psychic," and she had a supporting role. But Raven was so great and so captivating that they rewrote the show with her in the lead. "Raven sparkled and overshadowed everybody. She was the show," says director Sean McNamara. "She learned some things from Cosby. Her comedic timing is perfect. She totally gets it. She reads a script once and knows where to go and when to pause and when to nail the joke." She actually helps out the writers with teen slang, offering what she calls a "hip-hop-ictionary."

Raven looks forward to doing the series for several years. She says that in the second season her character gets a boyfriend "and gets into a lot more crazy things — but it's hilarious!" Is she like the character she plays? "I'm not as vibrant as she is," says the real Raven. "Her hyperness takes a lot out of me. I don't make my own clothes, but we both love to shop. Our love for friends and family are the same. I also have a best girlfriend and a best guy friend."

With the success of "That's So Raven," some observers have suggested that Disney seems to be grooming Raven as its next It Girl, in line with Hilary Duff and Lizzie McGuire. "Lizzie was on for a year and a half before it exploded," said Disney Channel entertainment president Rich Ross. "Raven was on for six months. We expect her to be a big star for this company." As industry analyst Lily Oei remarked, "Her quick rise may herald a new era at the network, one with a curvy, sassy black girl as its poster child."

The Cheetah Girls

In the summer of 2003, Raven appeared in the made-for-TV movie *The Cheetah Girls*, based on the popular series of books by Deborah Gregory. Raven played Galleria Garibaldi, a fashion queen who's trying to get her girl group to win the high school talent show. The other three characters in this urban fairy tale are Chanel (played by Adrienne Bailon), Aqua (played by Kiely Williams), and Dorinda (played by Sabrina Bryan); both Adrienne and Kiely are actually in the teen pop/hip-hop group 3LW.

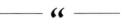

"Raven sparkled and overshadowed everybody. She was the show," says director Sean McNamara. "She learned some things from Cosby. Her comedic timing is perfect. She totally gets it. She reads a script once and knows where to go and when to pause and when to nail the joke."

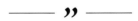

Raven loved appearing in *The Cheetah Girls*. "The first thing that attracted me to the role is that I got to act, sing, and dance," she says. She also loved the clothes, the hair, and the fancy makeup. But it was her charm and comedic skills that caught many viewers' attention. "She reminds me of Bea [Arthur], Gilda [Radner], and Carol [Burnett]," says Disney president Rich Ross. "Raven's in their league. She's fearless." Raven just shrugs off such compliments: "I'm very comfortable with what I do. I like entertaining people and making them laugh."

The Cheetah Girls debuted on Disney in August 2003; the studio also released a soundtrack CD with music from the film. The movie received

Raven with the Cheetah Girls.

mixed reviews from critics. Many praised Raven's performance while criticizing the film overall, as in this remark from *Daily Variety*: "Ironically, *Cheetah Girls* supposedly denounces manufactured pop music and marketing over artistry, yet it plays like a two-hour fashion commercial and culminates in a ridiculous lip-synching extravaganza." But viewers seemed to love it, and the movie earned great ratings. It was a top-ranked show when it was first broadcast, prompting Disney to replay it later that month with an alternate ending and 12 extra minutes of footage.

EDUCATION

Throughout her performing career, Raven has mixed being tutored on the set with attending a regular public school in Atlanta. From the late 1990s until she started work on "That's So Raven," she was able to have several years of a normal teenage life, going to class at North Springs High School, shopping, and having sleepovers with her friends. But when "That's So Raven" started, it was back to the challenges of working and learning on the set. She says that kids in her position should be appreciated for all their hard work. "Hey, you know, adults need to give the kids in this business more credit, because we have to be on the set, plus three hours of school, so we have to know the whole script, plus the War of 1812 and take a test on it."

Raven graduated from North Springs in Atlanta in the fall of 2003, and she plans to go to college in a few years. She's now based in California, and she hopes to attend either UCLA or USC in the future. "Hopefully, I will stay in the business," she says, "but it's very flaky and you never know if you're going to get a job. So when I go to college, what I major in is going to be something different than acting, just in case it doesn't work out." Raven also loves to cook, and she'd like to go to culinary school, too, and maybe open her own restaurant someday.

FUTURE PLANS

Right now, Raven is working on several new movies and new records. She's slated to appear in the film *All-American Girl*, based on the book by Meg Cabot; she plays a girl who saves the president's life. She'll also appear in *Sparkle*, a movie about a girl group similar to the Supremes. She's working on her third album and on a soundtrack for the "That's So Raven" show. She says she's open to all kinds of new roles. "I want to do everything," she says. "I want to do a 'dramedy' and mix the comedy and drama all up."

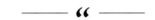

Even though she's been in show business for 15 years, Raven will always be Olivia to some fans. "People are funny," she laughs. "They'll come up to me and they're like, 'You look like the girl in 'The Cosby Show,' but you're not her because she's three.' And I'm like, 'That was 14 years ago!'"

Even though she's been in show business for 15 years, Raven will always be Olivia to some fans. "People are funny," she laughs. "They'll come up to me and they're like, 'You look like the girl in 'The Cosby Show,' but you're not her because she's three.' And I'm like, 'That was 14 years ago!'"

HOME AND FAMILY

Raven still lives with her family, and they split their time between a home in Atlanta and one in California, near the studios. She's very close to her family, and says they help her stay grounded. "I mean, I have to clean my room," she says. In her spare time, she likes to hang out with friends, shop, and listen to all kinds of music. She also likes to paint.

Raven is active in many charities, including Colin Powell's Children First program, the Paralympics, the March of Dimes, DARE, Juvenile Diabetes, Pediatric AIDS, and the Ronald McDonald Houses. She's also a spokeswoman for Disney's Adventure All-Star volunteer program, and she encourages kids to help out in their own communities. "Kids especially need to try to make a difference, because we're going to have to run this world one day," she says. "We don't want to live in a world where everyone's mad at each other or where there's dirt everywhere. We want to make it better."

Raven is also something of a role model for girls who have curves. She doesn't have a thin, model-like body. "I have a little tummy-tummy," she says. "I do my crunches. I'm muscular. My girls know I like to eat." At one point, she thought her shape might prevent her from getting good roles, because most TV and movie actresses are very thin. But it didn't stop her from getting starring roles in "That's So Raven" and *The Cheetah Girls*, and now she's proud to look the way she does. "The other teenage stars out there today, are, like, puny," she says. "Don't get me wrong, they look great. But I can't get that small. I'm telling my girls it's okay." She says she might like to have her own line of clothes someday, too. "If I was to do my own clothing line, I would do it for girls who are built like me. When I shop for myself it's very hard to find clothes. I'm curvy and there should be more clothes for curvy girls."

"

"The other teenage stars out there today, are, like, puny," Raven says. "Don't get me wrong, they look great. But I can't get that small. I'm telling my girls it's okay." She says she might like to have her own line of clothes someday, too. *"If I was to do my own clothing line, I would do it for girls who are built like me. When I shop for myself it's very hard to find clothes. I'm curvy and there should be more clothes for curvy girls."*

"

CREDITS

Television

"The Cosby Show," 1989-92 (TV series)
Queen, 1993 (TV movie)
"Hangin' with Mr. Cooper," 1993-97 (TV series)
Zenon: Girl of the 21st Century, 1999 (TV movie)
"Kim Possible," 2002- (TV series)
"That's So Raven," 2003- (TV series)
The Cheetah Girls, 2003 (TV movie)

Movies

The Little Rascals, 1994
Dr. Doolittle, 1998
Dr. Doolittle 2, 2001

Recordings

Here's to New Dreams, 1993
Undeniable, 1999
The Cheetah Girls, 2003

FURTHER READING

Books

Who's Who Among African Americans, 2003

Periodicals

Atlanta Journal-Constitution, Apr. 29, 1996, p.B3; May 31, 1999, p.C6
Bergen County (NJ) Record, June 22, 2001, p.5
Boston Globe, Jan. 16, 2003, p.D5
Boston Herald, Jan. 16, 2003, Arts and Life section, p.41
Chicago Tribune, Dec. 13, 1994, Kidnews, p.1
Daily News, Aug. 11, 2003, Television section, p.85
Detroit Free Press, Sep. 11, 2003, Yak's Corner, p.4
Ebony, May 1990, p.106
Entertainment Weekly, Oct. 17, 2003, p.42
Essence, Oct. 3, 2003, p.148
Houston Chronicle, June 25, 1998, p.5
Jet, Apr. 2, 1990, p.22; May 20, 1991, p.54; Nov. 8, 1993, p.58; Sep. 8, 2003, p.60
Los Angeles Times, Jan. 17, 2003, Part 5, p.2
Newsday, June 9, 1991, Part II, p.4; May 30, 1993, Part II, p.1; Oct. 19, 2003, Kidsday, p.1
New York Post, June 23, 2001, p.21
New York Times, Jan. 12, 2003, p.59
Philadelphia Tribune, Mar. 30, 1999, p.B4
People, June 26, 2000, p.68; May 20, 2002, p.140
Teen People, Feb. 1, 2004, p.93
Toronto Sun, Nov. 26, 2002, Entertainment, p.60
USA Today, Oct. 26, 1989, p.D3
USA Weekend, Aug. 8-10, 2003, p.6

Online Articles

http://www.timeforkids.com
    (*Time for Kids*, "Who's News," Aug. 20, 2003)

Online Database

Biography Resource Center Online, article from *Who's Who Among African Americans,* 2003

ADDRESS

Raven
Disney Channel
3800 West Almeda Avenue
Burbank, CA 91505

WORLD WIDE WEB SITE

http://psc.disney.go.com/disneychannel/thassoraven

Will Wright 1960-

American Game Designer
Creator of the Best-Selling Computer Games
"SimCity," "The Sims," and "The Sims Online"

BIRTH

William R. Wright was born on January 20, 1960, in Atlanta, Georgia, to William (Bill) Wright, a chemical engineer and owner of Wright Plastics Company, and Beverly Edwards, a community theater actress. Will had one sister. When he was nine years old, his father died. Seeking the support of her family, Will's mother moved with her children to her hometown of Baton Rouge, Louisiana, where Will lived until he was 18.

YOUTH

Wright was a bright and motivated child. He read widely from an early age and once described his appetite for knowledge as "obsessive." "I would usually get very obsessed with some subject or area of interest for six months or a year, and just totally learn everything I (could) about it."

For fun, Wright loved to play board games, especially chess, a Chinese game named "Go," and complex military strategy and historical war games. Wright ranked "Go" as his favorite game because its two simple rules "give rise to incredible strategy."

Wright "always associated fun with making something." He spent hours building toy models of airplanes, ships, and tanks. "I was always building things," he remembered. From toy models, he moved on to robots. His first, built when he was 13, was a hydraulic arm created out of injection syringes.

Wright read widely from an early age and once described his appetite for knowledge as "obsessive." "I would usually get very obsessed with some subject or area of interest for six months or a year, and just totally learn everything I (could) about it."

EDUCATION

Although Wright was smart, he didn't fit well within the confines of regular school. He sped through high school in three years, graduating at age 16. He began his university studies at Louisiana State University, but soon transferred to Louisiana Tech, and then to the New School University in New York. Five years of college work — during which he studied architecture, mechanical engineering, aviation, brain physiology, and psychology — left him with no degree and no interest in continuing school. He dropped out in 1981. He had fallen in love with an artist named Joell Jones and moved to live with her in California.

Dropping out of college didn't stop Wright's active mind — he had never needed school to motivate him to learn. His interest in his own projects continued unabated; he earned his pilot's license and became a minister. But his greatest obsession became the computer. At age 20, the

> ———— " ————
>
> *The computers that appeared on the market beginning in the late 1970s allowed programmers to type code directly into a personal computer and to test their programs instantly. Wright was delighted. "Once I got my hands on my first PC, I became totally enamored with it," he recalled.*
>
> ———— " ————

year before leaving his college studies, Wright played a flight simulator game produced by Bruce Artwick Productions. The life-like experience portrayed on the computer screen fascinated Wright.

Although the game captured his interest, Wright didn't immediately get hooked on computer programming. When he took computer programming courses in college, programming was done by creating hundreds or even thousands of punched cardboard cards (called keypunch cards), which were fed into a large mainframe computer. Keypunch cards made programming a very slow, laborious process, and Wright hated it. But advances in computer technology soon helped foster his interest in programming. The computers that appeared on the market beginning in the late 1970s allowed programmers to type code directly into a personal computer and to test their programs instantly. Wright was delighted. "Once I got my hands on my first PC, I became totally enamored with it," he recalled. With his Apple II computer, Wright could write a program and immediately test the results. He first used it to animate the robots that he continued to build as a hobby. "I was very interested in the idea of animating inanimate objects," he remembered. One of his first computer-controlled robots, Mr. Rogers, was a three-wheeled creation that mapped the rooms in his house with ultrasonic sensors that radioed data back to his computer.

By age 22, Wright discovered the Commodore 64 personal computer and perfected his computer programming skills enough to develop his first game, "Raid on Bungeling Bay." The game was simple: a player pilots a helicopter over islands and blows things up. In Wright's opinion, however, it was "a very stupid game."

FIRST JOBS

Despite Wright's opinion, "Raid on Bungeling Bay" became his first success. In 1982, Wright presented his game to a software distribution company, which immediately agreed to distribute it. "I walked in the door and they said 'Oh great, we'll take it.' I didn't have to talk them into it," Wright remembered. "Raid on Bungeling Bay" became one of the first computer games exported from America to Japan. Although not very popular in the United States, it sold 800,000 copies in Japan alone. The market response stunned Wright. "I was amazed I could make a living at this," he recalled. "It was something I was willing to do for free."

But Wright discovered a glitch in his plan to become a game developer while making "Raid on Bungeling Bay." He'd had more fun building the city that was destroyed — the landscape, roads, and buildings — than he did flying the helicopter around bombing targets. Instead of creating another destruction oriented game, the kind of game that dominated the market in the mid-1980s, Wright dove into an intensive research project that would ultimately result in the creation of "SimCity," the game that set him apart from all other game developers.

CAREER HIGHLIGHTS

To flesh out the details for his new game about building a city, Wright read about 20 books on urban planning theory, especially the work of MIT electrical engineering professor Jay W. Forrester, author of *Urban Dynamics*. Wright also researched computer simulation techniques. He created a game based on land use, traffic, power distribution systems, and other urban development structure research conducted in the late 1960s and 1970s. He called his game prototype "Metropolis."

"Raid on Bungeling Bay" became one of the first computer games exported from America to Japan. Although not very popular in the United States, it sold 800,000 copies in Japan alone. The market response stunned Wright. "I was amazed I could make a living at this," he recalled. "It was something I was willing to do for free."

Wright's research resulted in a game that offered players a job as mayor of a virtual city. Players took responsibility for building houses and roads, attracting businesses, raising taxes, and keeping the citizens happy. Depending on the player's skill, Simulated Citizens (or Sims) either moved into the city to build homes, businesses, hospitals, schools, and churches, or moved out to search for a better place to live. The player decided how to define success in the game. For one player, success might mean a prosperous city with good schools, low crime, and no traffic, while another player might define success in the game as a decaying city that Sims tried to escape. The game could be played differently each time.

Unlike other games on the market at the time, "Metropolis" had no winner, no loser, no hero, no enemies, no bloody attacks, and no end. And no game publisher wanted to market it, either. Discouraged, Wright shelved "Metropolis" until Jeff Braun enticed him to unpack it in 1987.

―――― *"* ――――

"SimCity" piqued the interest of both domestic and foreign governmental agencies, including the Central Intelligence Agency and the Defense Department. Large businesses wondered how the idea of simulation might aid their training programs and other goals. In addition, "SimCity" gained attention as an educational tool and made its way into more than 10,000 classrooms.

―――― *"* ――――

"SimCity"

Jeff Braun would soon become integral to the development of Wright's game. At the time, Braun was working for a video-game distributor in California. But he'd grown tired of working for someone else and was looking for a way to enter the video gaming industry himself. Braun invited Wright and some other game developers to a pizza party at his home near San Francisco in 1987. At the party, Wright described his shelved game to Braun. Intrigued, Braun asked to see it. Once Braun looked at Wright's game, he "went ballistic," as he told *Time*. "I knew immediately," he recalled. Convinced that Wright's game would be a success, Braun persuaded Wright to stop his worrying that "no one likes it."

Braun and Wright soon formed Maxis Studios in Walnut Creek, California. For the next two years Braun, Wright, and a handful of developers worked out of Braun's apartment. They used the living room for programming, the kitchen as a mail room, and one bedroom as an administrative office. Maxis struck a deal with Broderbund, one of the largest game companies in America, to distribute the game. "SimCity" debuted in stores in 1989, and it became an instant success. *Newsweek* featured it in a full-page review, which gave the game national publicity and helped sales soar. By the end of the year sales had reached $3 million.

As the popularity of "SimCity" grew, Wright's creation piqued the interest of both domestic and foreign governmental agencies, including the Central

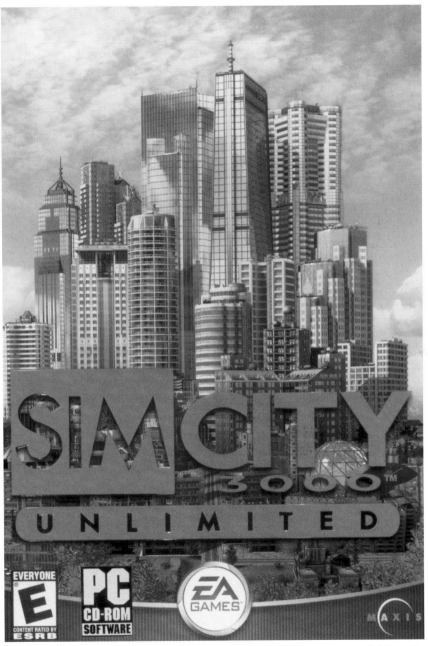

The original "SimCity" game in 1989 eventually led to a very successful line of related games, including "SimCity 3000," the top-selling game of 1999.

Intelligence Agency and the Defense Department. Large businesses wondered how the idea of simulation might aid their training programs and other goals. In addition, "SimCity" gained attention as an educational tool and made its way into more than 10,000 classrooms. By 1995 Maxis had grown to a company of almost 300 employees with sales of $38.1 million.

As interest in the game continued, Wright did more research to improve the game experience. He interviewed city planners, police administrators, public works officials, and others to create new editions and expansion packs to enhance the original game. While the enhancements did not change the structure of the game, they enabled players to customize the look of their cities with terrain from samples from the 48 contiguous United States, ward off disasters based on both reality and fantasy, and customize the architectural styles of their buildings, among other things. "Sim-City 3000" became the top-selling game of 1999, adding tornadoes and UFO attacks to the game. By 2003 the various versions of "SimCity" had won more than 24 awards.

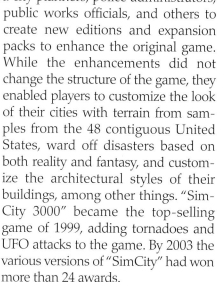

"Some subject that I'm reading about ... will pique my interest and then I'll slowly become obsessed with it," Wright explained about his design process. "I've always liked studying different things. That's one reason why I really like doing game design. It gives me an excuse to go out and research these wildly different things for a year or two and then move onto the next thing later."

Creating Games in the "Sim" Series

Keen to repeat the success of "Sim-City," Maxis supported the development of other games in the "Sim" series. In 1990 "SimEarth — The Living Planet" debuted, becoming a bestseller by 1991; "SimAnt — The Electronic Ant Colony" came out in 1991; "SimFarm" hit the stores in 1993; and "SimCopter" and "SimPark," among others, debuted in 1996.

Each new game was sparked by Wright's love of reading. "Some subject that I'm reading about . . . will pique my interest and then I'll slowly become obsessed with it," he explained about his design process. "I've always liked studying different things. That's one reason why I really like doing game design. It gives me an excuse to go out and research these wildly different things for a year or two and then move onto the next thing later."

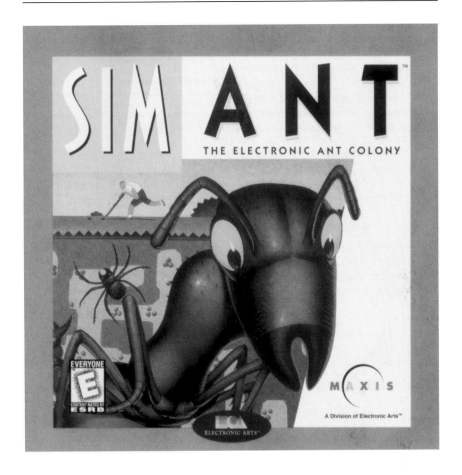

Indeed, the "Sim" series of games did have vastly different sources of inspiration. "SimEarth" developed from Wright's interest in James Lovelock's Gaia theory, which emphasizes the interconnectedness of all Earth's living matter and their planet's atmosphere. Players create a whole planet by setting the planet's evolutionary timescale, geological features, and environmental conditions. From these set points, life forms develop. Players can manage their planet to create intelligent life forms and civilizations, which give rise to the development of technology. Some of the dangers to the players' creations are such natural disasters as earthquakes or volcanic explosions or competitive problems that lead to the outbreak of wars. "SimAnt" was inspired by the work of Edward O. Wilson, a Harvard entomologist. (For more information on Wilson, see *Biography Today Scientists & Inventors*, Vol. 8.) With co-author Bert Hölldobler, Wilson detailed the history, evolution, social structures, and communication of ants in *The Ants*,

177

"The Sims" games include scenes like these from "The Sims Superstar Expansion Pack."

for which they won the Pulitzer Prize for non-fiction in 1991. Wright used their research to develop a game in which players control the life of an ant colony.

The diverse subjects of these games indicate, as Jeff Braun told *Wired*, that Wright is "a perpetual student." His friend Bruce Joffe, a geographic information systems consultant, once said that "Everything about life interests Will; he has a childlike fascination. . . . [He] drinks information in, synthesizes it, and then creates something useful out of it." Wright recognizes his own intensity, saying that "I typically go overboard when I research new projects." But his ability to translate the vast knowledge he gathers into games enjoyed by both children and adults has transformed the computer game market.

The "Sim" series of games offered players an experience unlike any other games. "With most games, the game itself is the constraint on what you can do," Wright explained. "In 'Doom,' you can't go up to the monsters and ask them why they're trying to kill you, and if there's a wall, you can't climb over it. Behaviors are very regular and predictable." Instead, Wright's games contrasted with these shoot, chase, and kill games by offering players the chance to explore and be creative. The *Los Angeles Times* pinned the success of his games on his ability to create "realistic simulations, which previously had been available only to scientists and the military, to home computers." As Wright explained, his games offer players "something less like a slide—where you can do one fun thing over and over—and more like a sandbox."

> *"With most games, the game itself is the constraint on what you can do," Wright explained. "In 'Doom,' you can't go up to the monsters and ask them why they're trying to kill you, and if there's a wall, you can't climb over it. Behaviors are very regular and predictable."*

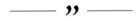

Struggles to Repeat Success

"SimCity" was a huge market success with correspondingly high profit levels. The desire to maintain these profit levels put pressure on Maxis. The company had grown very quickly to support "SimCity." But when its sales began to level off, Maxis found it difficult to reach its earlier profit levels. The company had so many employees that just paying salaries left the company with few resources for game research. Instead of original games, Maxis employees rushed to create "SimCity" spin-offs in order to keep a steady flow of income. But the games that Maxis hastily sent to market were less and less appealing to customers. By 1996 Maxis posted a loss of $1.7 million. Instead of trying to churn out more games, Maxis began accepting acquisition offers. One of the largest American game publishers, Electronic Arts (EA) of Redwood City, California, bought Maxis in 1996 for $125 million. EA immediately laid off 40 percent of the Maxis employees in order to refocus the company for success. But it also offered Maxis the financial support it needed to take the time to create best-selling games.

When EA took over Maxis, it soon realized that Wright's design ideas had been abandoned by Maxis. Wright was working on his own ideas with almost no help or money from Maxis. "We saw a hall-of-fame designer who wanted to do crazy stuff everyone knew couldn't be done," said the executive vice president and chief creative officer from Electronic Arts. "We thought, 'Let's help him.'" EA assembled a team to brainstorm with Wright.

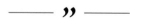

> *Wright had been working on a game he called "doll house." "Kids build a story around what they are doing. The doll house becomes the scaffolding to hold up their story. It's a place for them to think about or play roles of the person they would like to be," Wright said. His game provided players with the "props and sets and actors, and the idea is to build a story."*

"The Sims"

Wright had been working on a game he called "dollhouse" since 1994. As he described it, instead of dealing with a larger world, this new idea took "'SimCity' to the level of the individual." Instead of a whole city, the game would focus on the minute details of the home. One book in particular influenced his thinking about the game: *A Pattern Language* by Christopher Alexander, who laid out an architectural theory based on function rather than form. Alexander described a way for people to "score" building plans that Wright incorporated into his game design.

Wright wanted his game to allow people to design their perfect home with feedback on the success of their design from game characters who inhabited the house. While creating the perfect home began as the object of the game, Wright quickly realized that the characters, or Sims, were more interesting than the architecture, and he shifted the game's focus to the time management and activities involved in normal daily life.

The perfect home became the stage for people to play with everyday life. "Kids build a story around what they are doing. The doll house becomes the scaffolding to hold up their story. It's a place for them to think about or play roles of the person they would like to be," Wright said. His game provided players with the "props and sets and actors, and the idea is to build a story." The game developed so that Sim characters have emotional and biological needs, just like real people. The Sim characters have personality

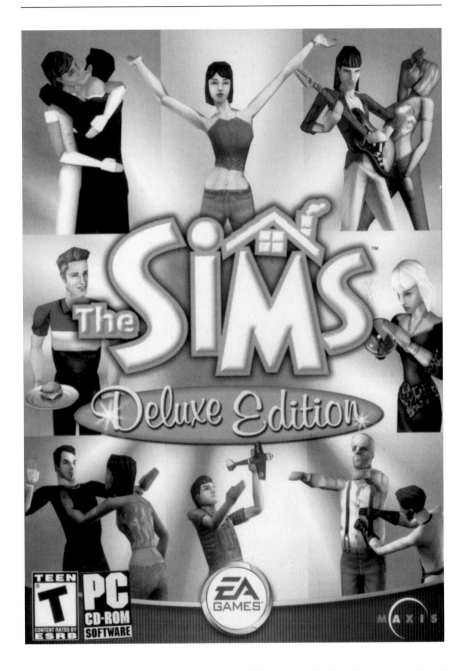

traits, including Neat, Outgoing, Active, Playful, and Nice. Players set Sims' characteristics then manage their virtual lives, helping them build homes, find jobs, and make friends. Players must also make sure the Sims eat, get plenty of rest, wash, and take regular restroom breaks. Players can struc-

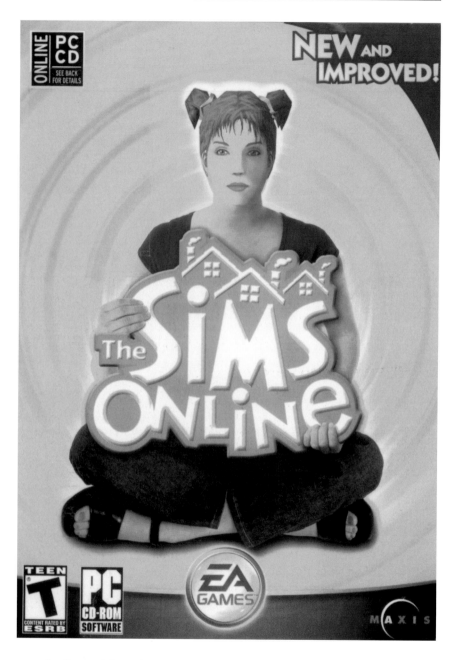

ture the lives of Sim characters any way they like. If players attend to their characters' needs, Sims go to work, keep their house in order, make friends or fall in love, and even have babies. If players neglect their Sims' needs, the characters fall ill, get depressed, lose their jobs, get divorced, or have their babies taken away by social services. Wright enjoyed the open-ended nature of the game, saying "I think that letting the players choose their goals and pursue them gives the game so much re-playability and also allows the players to be so much more creative with what they do in the game."

Released in 2000, "The Sims" became the top-grossing computer game the same year. Expansion packs quickly followed that enabled Sims to go on dates, own pets, vacation on tropical beaches or at fancy resorts, host costume parties, and dance at nightclubs, among other things. By 2001 "The Sims" and four of its expansion packs were among the top 10 best-selling computer games in the United States. In 2002, "The Sims" became the best-selling computer game of all time. *Entertainment Weekly* named "The Sims" one of the 100 greatest computer games of all time in 2003, by which time eight million copies of the game and almost 16 million expansion packs had been sold. "Reaction to 'The Sims' by both customers and critics have exceeded our most ambitious expectations," said EA president John Riccitiello. "'The Sims' has become a cultural phenomenon. Its worldwide appeal spans hard-core gamers, casual computer users, and even gaming's most elusive group of consumers, women. Over 50 percent of new 'Sims' players are female."

As Lev Grossman wrote in Time *magazine, "Experiencing 'The Sims Online' is less like playing a game than taking part in an open-ended community theater production, where the dialogue is improvised, the theme is modern life, and the star is you."*

"The Sims" Move Online

With such success, Wright imagined "The Sims" on yet another level: online. Instead of interacting with preset programs, players would interact with each other over the Internet. "The Sims Online" launched in 2002 after more than a year of feedback from 38,000 online test players. Wright and his team created the game so that each Sim character represents a real individual. The characters have the power to create their own communities together, marry each other, share houses, and even build businesses and political systems. As Lev Grossman wrote in *Time* magazine, "Experiencing 'The Sims Online' is less like playing a game than taking part in an open-ended community theater production, where the dialogue is improvised, the theme is modern life, and the star is you." By 2004, "The Sims Online" had attracted several thousand players.

Game players create and control characters like these from "The Sims Superstar Expansion Pack."

What makes this game different from other online multi-player games is that players' successes are measured by the happiness of other people. One of the designers of "The Sims Online," Gordon Watson, said that the game will allow people to interact "on a pure intellectual and emotional level." But Wright admitted that the idea scared him, saying "we're building something that could potentially be a very powerful experience for a lot of people. So it's an opportunity as well as a danger. Realistically, I think this game is going to be a tremendous help for a lot of people and tremendously bad for a lot of people. I just wonder what the net is going to be."

When asked by the *Los Angeles Times* if he thought he might push the boundaries of interactive entertainment too far, Wright replied: "I'm not sure what too far would be. Interactive entertainment's a relatively new medium. . . . This industry resembles the Wild West. Nobody know the rules; we're trying to figure things out by doing them. I'd be more worried about not going far enough."

Beyond "The Sims"

When Wright isn't working on his computer games, he concentrates on having fun in other ways. He founded the Stupid Fun Club, a think tank for fun ideas. Housed in a 3,800 square-foot warehouse in Berkeley, California, the Stupid Fun Club has two full-time workers and several part-time employees helping Wright come up with ideas for films and television. In 2003, he contracted with the Fox Network to develop new, innovative ideas for television. With his partners Michael Winter and Marc Thorpe, who work with him at the Stupid Fun Club studio, Wright developed an animated show called "M.Y. Robot" and a reality-based show in which people would be filmed reacting to a life-size, remote-controlled robot. About the new projects, Mike Darnell, head of alternative programming for Fox, told the *Hollywood Reporter* that "Clearly, Will's a genius . . .

so we decided to give him a basic development deal and see what he comes up with." Indeed, with Wright's diverse interests, it will be interesting to see what he develops.

Advice for Future Game Designers

When asked for advice for those who would like to follow in his footsteps as a game designer, Wright offered these words of wisdom: "Be patient. Hit games can take years. It's easy to get frustrated. Maintain your passion. It's the biggest indicator of eventual success."

When asked for advice for those who would like to follow in his footsteps as a game designer, Wright offered these words of wisdom: "Be patient. Hit games can take years. It's easy to get frustrated. Maintain your passion. It's the biggest indicator of eventual success."

MARRIAGE AND FAMILY

Wright met his wife, Joell Jones, in Louisiana while spending one summer between college courses at home. Jones remembered that summer, saying "We'd fallen madly in love. I'm 12 years older . . . so there was that age difference, but we couldn't drop it." Within a year, Wright dropped out of college and moved to California, where Jones worked as an artist. The couple remains happily married in California; their daughter, Cassidy, was born in 1986.

Wright says his wife is "probably the most computer illiterate person" he knows. "She's never played any of my games. That's probably why we get along so well." But Cassidy shares her father's interest in technology. Wright has implemented Cassidy's suggestions for his games since she was five, when she requested an option for frogs to rule the planet in "SimEarth." One of her most sweeping suggestions was to base "Sims" characters in their homes, not their workplaces. After trying a prototype of the game, Cassidy realized that "What was interesting was the people, not what they did for a living," she told *Teen People*. She also suggested that "The Sims" game include more opportunities for shopping, since teenagers enjoy hanging out at the mall.

HOBBIES AND OTHER INTERESTS

Wright's interest in the hobby he began as a 13 year old has lasted. He continues to create robots in his spare time and has nurtured his daughter's interest in the same hobby. Cassidy has designed robots with her father since 1994. The two have competed in BattleBots robotic competitions (which were shown on the cable network Comedy Central). Father and daughter share a sense of humor as well, giving their creations such names as "Kitty Puff Puff," "Misty the WonderBot," and "ChiaBot," instead of the menacing names of their competitors, "Battle Scar" and "Dawn of Destruction."

SELECTED HONORS AND AWARDS

The Time Digital 50 (Time.com): 1999
Invisionary Award (NewMedia Invision Festival): 2000
GDC Game of the Year Award: 2001, for "The Sims"
Lifetime Achievement Award (Gama Network and the International Game Developers Association): 2001
Inducted into the Academy of Interactive Arts and Sciences Hall of Fame: 2002
Champion Award (Interactive Digital Software Association): 2002

FURTHER READING

Periodicals

Computer Gaming World, May 2000, p.64
Contra Costa (Calif.) Times, Feb. 18, 2001, p.C1
Current Biography, Feb. 2004
Entertainment Weekly, Dec. 6, 2002, p.38
Esquire, Dec. 2002, p.146
Forbes, May 28, 2001, p.12
Los Angeles Times, Oct. 19, 2000, p.T12; May 17, 2001, p.T2
New York Times Magazine, Oct. 31, 1999, p.24
Newsweek, Oct. 24, 1994, p.48; Nov. 25, 2002, p.53
PC Magazine, May 14, 2002
San Francisco Examiner, May 8, 1994, p.C1
Time, Feb. 19, 1996; Nov. 25, 2002, p.78
Washington Post, Apr. 14, 2002, magazine section, p.W8
Wired, Nov. 2002, p.176

Online Articles

http://www.cnn.com/COMMUNITY/transcripts/2000/12/1/wright.chat/ (*CNN.com,* "Will Wright on Creating 'The Sims' and 'SimCity,'" Nov. 30, 2000)

http://www.firstmonday.dk/issues/issue4_4/friedman/
  (*First Monday,* "Semiotics of SimCity," 1999)
http://www.gamespot.com/features/maxis/index.html
  (*Gamespot.com,* "SIMply Divine," undated)
http://www.gamespot.com/gamespot/features/pc/simsonline/index.html
  (*Gamespot.com,* "The Endless Hours of The Sims Online," undated)
http://www.gamespot.com/gamespot/features/pc/simsonline/1.html
  (*Gamespot.com,* "The Back-Burner Blockbuster,"undated)
http://www.prospect.org/print-friendly/print/V5/17/starr-p.html
  (*American Prospect,* "Seductions of Sim," Mar. 21, 1994)

Online Databases

Biography Resource Center Online, 2003, article from *Newsmakers,* 2003

ADDRESS

Will Wright
Electronic Arts/Maxis
2121 North California Boulevard
Walnut Creek, CA 94596

WORLD WIDE WEB SITES

http://www.maxis.com

Photo and Illustration Credits

Tony Blair/Photos: Patrick Kovarik/AFP/Getty Images; copyright © CORBIS Sygma; copyright © Royalty-Free/CORBIS; copyright © Polak Matthew/ CORBIS Sygma (pp. 17, 19); AP/Wide World Photos; Mike Theiler/Getty Images; AP/Wide World Photos. Front cover: Paul O'Driscoll/Bloomberg News/Landov.

Kim Clijsters/Photos: AP/Wide World Photos; Ian Waldie/Reuters; Al Bello/ Getty Images; Jeff Gross/Getty Images (p. 37); AP/Wide World Photos; Greg Wood/AFP/Getty Images.

Celia Cruz/Photos: AP/Wide World Photos; Reuters/Landov; Deborah Fein-gold/Getty Images; copyright © Emerson Sam/CORBIS; AP/Wide World Photos. Album/CD covers: CANCIONES PREMIADAS copyright © & (p) 1989. Palladium-Latin Jazz and Dance Records. Licensed by Met Richmond Records Inc. for West Side Latino; LA INCOMPARABLE CELIA copyright © & (p) 1989. Palladium-Latin Jazz and Dance Records. Licensed by Met Richmond Records Inc. for West Side Latino; REGALO DEL ALMA (p) 2003, 2000 Sony Music Entertainment Inc. Copyright © 2003 Sony Music Entertainment Inc.

The Donnas/Photos: copyright © Chapman Baehler/Retna; copyright © Jay Blakesberg/Retna; AP/Wide World Photos. CD covers: AMERICAN TEENAGE ROCK 'N' ROLL MACHINE copyright © & (p) 1998 Look-out!; THE DONNAS copyright © & (p) 1998 Lookout! Records LLC; THE DONNAS TURN 21 copyright © & (p) 2001 Lookout! Records LLC; GET SKINTIGHT copyright © 1999 Lookout! Records LLC; SPEND THE NIGHT copyright © 2002 Atlantic Recording Corporation for the United States and WEA International Inc. for the world outside the United States.

Tim Duncan/Photos: Andrew D. Bernstein/NBAE/Getty Images; Rick Stew-art/Getty Images; Doug Pensinger/Getty Images; AP/Wide World Photos; Todd Warshaw/Getty Images; AP/Wide World Photos.

Shirin Ebadi/Photos: Jack Guez/AFP/Getty Images; copyright © Attar Ma-her/CORBIS Sygma; AP/Wide World Photos; Atta Kenare/AFP/Getty Images; Odd Andersen/AFP/Getty Images (pp. 115, 116); copyright © France Keyser/In Visu/CORBIS.

How to Use the Cumulative Index

Our indexes have a new look. In an effort to make our indexes easier to use, we've combined the Name and General Index into a new, Cumulative Index. This single ready-reference resource covers all the volumes in *Biography Today*, both the general series and the special subject series. The new Cumulative Index contains complete listings of all individuals who have appeared in *Biography Today* since the series began. Their names appear in bold-faced type, followed by the issue in which they appear. The Cumulative Index also includes references for the occupations, nationalities, and ethnic and minority origins of individuals profiled in *Biography Today*.

We have also made some changes to our specialty indexes, the Places of Birth Index and the Birthday Index. To consolidate and to save space, the Places of Birth Index and the Birthday Index will no longer appear in the January and April issues of the softbound subscription series. But these indexes can still be found in the September issue of the softbound subscription series, in the hardbound Annual Cumulation at the end of each year, and in each volume of the special subject series.

General Series

The General Series of *Biography Today* is denoted in the index with the month and year of the issue in which the individual appeared. Each individual also appears in the Annual Cumulation for that year.

Blair, Tony . . . . Apr 04
Bonds, Barry . . . . Jan 03
Bush, Laura . . . . Jan 03
Eminem . . . . Apr 03
Fox, Vicente . . . . Jan 03
Giuliani, Rudolph . . . . Sep 02
Hartnett, Josh . . . . Sep 03
Kutcher, Ashton . . . . Apr 04
Leslie, Lisa . . . . Jan 04
Mayer, John . . . . Apr 04
Rice, Condoleezza . . . . Apr 03
Reeves, Keanu . . . . Jan 04
Stefani, Gwen . . . . Sep 03
Tolkien, J.R.R. . . . . Jan 02
Witherspoon, Reese . . . . Apr 03

Special Subject Series

The Special Subject Series of *Biography Today* are each denoted in the index with an abbreviated form of the series name, plus the number of the volume in which the individual appears. They are listed as follows.

Adams, Ansel . . . . Artist V.1	(Artists)
Bloor, Edward . . . . Author V.15	(Authors)
Diaz, Cameron . . . . PerfArt V.3	(Performing Artists)
Fay, Michael . . . . Science V.9	(Scientists & Inventors)
Milbrett, Tiffeny . . . . Sport V.10	(Sports)
Peterson, Roger Tory . . . . WorLdr V.1	(World Leaders: Environmental Leaders)
Sadat, Anwar . . . . WorLdr V.2	(World Leaders: Modern African Leaders)
Wolf, Hazel. . . . . WorLdr V.3	(World Leaders: Environmental Leaders 2)

Updates

Updated information on selected individuals appears in the Appendix at the end of some issues of the *Biography Today* Annual Cumulation. In the index, the original entry is listed first, followed by any updates.

Arafat, Yasir . . . . Sep 94; Update 94;
  Update 95; Update 96; Update 97; Update 98;
  Update 00; Update 01; Update 02
Gates, Bill . . . . Apr 93; Update 98;
  Update 00; Science V.5; Update 01
Griffith Joyner, Florence. . . . . Sport V.1;
  Update 98
Sanders, Barry . . . . Sep 95; Update 99
Spock, Dr. Benjamin . . . . Sep 95; Update 98
Yeltsin, Boris . . . . Apr 92; Update 93;
  Update 95; Update 96; Update 98; Update 00

Cumulative Index

This cumulative index includes names, occupations, nationalities, and ethnic and minority origins that pertain to all individuals profiled in *Biography Today* since the debut of the series in 1992.

blacks

CUMULATIVE INDEX

Biography Today

General Series

"Biography Today will be useful in elementary and middle school libraries and in public library children's collections where there is a need for biographies of current personalities. High schools serving reluctant readers may also want to consider a subscription."
— *Booklist,* American Library Association

"Highly recommended for the young adult audience. Readers will delight in the accessible, energetic, tell-all style; teachers, librarians, and parents will welcome the clever format, intelligent and informative text. It should prove especially useful in motivating 'reluctant' readers or literate nonreaders."
— *MultiCultural Review*

"Written in a friendly, almost chatty tone, the profiles offer quick, objective information. While coverage of current figures makes Biography Today a useful reference tool, an appealing format and wide scope make it a fun resource to browse." — *School Library Journal*

"The best source for current information at a level kids can understand."
— Kelly Bryant, School Librarian, Carlton, OR

"Easy for kids to read. We love it! Don't want to be without it."
— Lynn McWhirter, School Librarian, Rockford, IL

B*iography Today* **General Series** includes a unique combination of current biographical profiles that teachers and librarians — and the readers themselves — tell us are most appealing. The **General Series** is available as a 3-issue subscription; hardcover annual cumulation; or subscription plus cumulation.

Within the **General Series**, your readers will find a variety of sketches about:

- Authors
- Musicians
- Political leaders
- Sports figures
- Movie actresses & actors
- Cartoonists
- Scientists
- Astronauts
- TV personalities
- and the movers & shakers in many other fields!

ONE-YEAR SUBSCRIPTION
- 3 softcover issues, 6" x 9"
- Published in January, April, and September
- 1-year subscription, $60
- 150 pages per issue
- 10 profiles per issue
- Contact sources for additional information
- Cumulative General, Places of Birth, and Birthday Indexes

HARDBOUND ANNUAL CUMULATION
- Sturdy 6" x 9" hardbound volume
- Published in December
- $62 per volume
- 450 pages per volume
- 25-30 profiles — includes all profiles found in softcover issues for that calendar year
- Cumulative General, Places of Birth, and Birthday Indexes
- Special appendix features current updates of previous profiles

SUBSCRIPTION AND CUMULATION COMBINATION
- $99 for 3 softcover issues plus the hardbound volume

233

1992

Paula Abdul
Andre Agassi
Kirstie Alley
Terry Anderson
Roseanne Arnold
Isaac Asimov
James Baker
Charles Barkley
Larry Bird
Judy Blume
Berke Breathed
Garth Brooks
Barbara Bush
George Bush
Fidel Castro
Bill Clinton
Bill Cosby
Diana, Princess of Wales
Shannen Doherty
Elizabeth Dole
David Duke
Gloria Estefan
Mikhail Gorbachev
Steffi Graf
Wayne Gretzky
Matt Groening
Alex Haley
Hammer
Martin Handford
Stephen Hawking
Hulk Hogan
Saddam Hussein
Lee Iacocca
Bo Jackson
Mae Jemison
Peter Jennings
Steven Jobs
Pope John Paul II
Magic Johnson
Michael Jordon
Jackie Joyner-Kersee
Spike Lee
Mario Lemieux
Madeleine L'Engle
Jay Leno
Yo-Yo Ma
Nelson Mandela
Wynton Marsalis
Thurgood Marshall
Ann Martin
Barbara McClintock
Emily Arnold McCully
Antonia Novello

Sandra Day O'Connor
Rosa Parks
Jane Pauley
H. Ross Perot
Luke Perry
Scottie Pippen
Colin Powell
Jason Priestley
Queen Latifah
Yitzhak Rabin
Sally Ride
Pete Rose
Nolan Ryan
H. Norman
   Schwarzkopf
Jerry Seinfeld
Dr. Seuss
Gloria Steinem
Clarence Thomas
Chris Van Allsburg
Cynthia Voigt
Bill Watterson
Robin Williams
Oprah Winfrey
Kristi Yamaguchi
Boris Yeltsin

1993

Maya Angelou
Arthur Ashe
Avi
Kathleen Battle
Candice Bergen
Boutros Boutros-Ghali
Chris Burke
Dana Carvey
Cesar Chavez
Henry Cisneros
Hillary Rodham Clinton
Jacques Cousteau
Cindy Crawford
Macaulay Culkin
Lois Duncan
Marian Wright Edelman
Cecil Fielder
Bill Gates
Sara Gilbert
Dizzy Gillespie
Al Gore
Cathy Guisewite
Jasmine Guy
Anita Hill
Ice-T
Darci Kistler

k.d. lang
Dan Marino
Rigoberta Menchu
Walter Dean Myers
Martina Navratilova
Phyllis Reynolds Naylor
Rudolf Nureyev
Shaquille O'Neal
Janet Reno
Jerry Rice
Mary Robinson
Winona Ryder
Jerry Spinelli
Denzel Washington
Keenen Ivory Wayans
Dave Winfield

1994

Tim Allen
Marian Anderson
Mario Andretti
Ned Andrews
Yasir Arafat
Bruce Babbitt
Mayim Bialik
Bonnie Blair
Ed Bradley
John Candy
Mary Chapin Carpenter
Benjamin Chavis
Connie Chung
Beverly Cleary
Kurt Cobain
F.W. de Klerk
Rita Dove
Linda Ellerbee
Sergei Fedorov
Zlata Filipovic
Daisy Fuentes
Ruth Bader Ginsburg
Whoopi Goldberg
Tonya Harding
Melissa Joan Hart
Geoff Hooper
Whitney Houston
Dan Jansen
Nancy Kerrigan
Alexi Lalas
Charlotte Lopez
Wilma Mankiller
Shannon Miller
Toni Morrison
Richard Nixon
Greg Norman
Severo Ochoa

River Phoenix
Elizabeth Pine
Jonas Salk
Richard Scarry
Emmitt Smith
Will Smith
Steven Spielberg
Patrick Stewart
R.L. Stine
Lewis Thomas
Barbara Walters
Charlie Ward
Steve Young
Kim Zmeskal

1995

Troy Aikman
Jean-Bertrand Aristide
Oksana Baiul
Halle Berry
Benazir Bhutto
Jonathan Brandis
Warren E. Burger
Ken Burns
Candace Cameron
Jimmy Carter
Agnes de Mille
Placido Domingo
Janet Evans
Patrick Ewing
Newt Gingrich
John Goodman
Amy Grant
Jesse Jackson
James Earl Jones
Julie Krone
David Letterman
Rush Limbaugh
Heather Locklear
Reba McEntire
Joe Montana
Cosmas Ndeti
Hakeem Olajuwon
Ashley Olsen
Mary-Kate Olsen
Jennifer Parkinson
Linus Pauling
Itzhak Perlman
Cokie Roberts
Wilma Rudolph
Salt 'N' Pepa
Barry Sanders
William Shatner
Elizabeth George
   Speare

Dr. Benjamin Spock
Jonathan Taylor
  Thomas
Vicki Van Meter
Heather Whitestone
Pedro Zamora

1996

Aung San Suu Kyi
Boyz II Men
Brandy
Ron Brown
Mariah Carey
Jim Carrey
Larry Champagne III
Christo
Chelsea Clinton
Coolio
Bob Dole
David Duchovny
Debbi Fields
Chris Galeczka
Jerry Garcia
Jennie Garth
Wendy Guey
Tom Hanks
Alison Hargreaves
Sir Edmund Hillary
Judith Jamison
Barbara Jordan
Annie Leibovitz
Carl Lewis
Jim Lovell
Mickey Mantle
Lynn Margulis
Iqbal Masih
Mark Messier
Larisa Oleynik
Christopher Pike
David Robinson
Dennis Rodman
Selena
Monica Seles
Don Shula
Kerri Strug
Tiffani-Amber Thiessen
Dave Thomas
Jaleel White

1997

Madeleine Albright
Marcus Allen
Gillian Anderson
Rachel Blanchard
Zachery Ty Bryan
Adam Ezra Cohen
Claire Danes
Celine Dion
Jean Driscoll
Louis Farrakhan
Ella Fitzgerald
Harrison Ford
Bryant Gumbel
John Johnson
Michael Johnson
Maya Lin
George Lucas
John Madden
Bill Monroe
Alanis Morissette
Sam Morrison
Rosie O'Donnell
Muammar el-Qaddafi
Christopher Reeve
Pete Sampras
Pat Schroeder
Rebecca Sealfon
Tupac Shakur
Tabitha Soren
Herbert Tarvin
Merlin Tuttle
Mara Wilson

1998

Bella Abzug
Kofi Annan
Neve Campbell
Sean Combs (Puff
  Daddy)
Dalai Lama (Tenzin
  Gyatso)
Diana, Princess of Wales
Leonardo DiCaprio
Walter E. Diemer
Ruth Handler
Hanson
Livan Hernandez
Jewel
Jimmy Johnson
Tara Lipinski
Jody-Anne Maxwell
Dominique Moceanu
Alexandra Nechita

Brad Pitt
LeAnn Rimes
Emily Rosa
David Satcher
Betty Shabazz
Kordell Stewart
Shinichi Suzuki
Mother Teresa
Mike Vernon
Reggie White
Kate Winslet

1999

Ben Affleck
Jennifer Aniston
Maurice Ashley
Kobe Bryant
Bessie Delany
Sadie Delany
Sharon Draper
Sarah Michelle Gellar
John Glenn
Savion Glover
Jeff Gordon
David Hampton
Lauryn Hill
King Hussein
Lynn Johnston
Shari Lewis
Oseola McCarty
Mark McGwire
Slobodan Milosevic
Natalie Portman
J. K. Rowling
Frank Sinatra
Gene Siskel
Sammy Sosa
John Stanford
Natalia Toro
Shania Twain
Mitsuko Uchida
Jesse Ventura
Venus Williams

2000

Christina Aguilera
K.A. Applegate
Lance Armstrong
Backstreet Boys
Daisy Bates
Harry Blackmun
George W. Bush
Carson Daly
Ron Dayne
Henry Louis Gates, Jr.
Doris Haddock
  (Granny D)
Jennifer Love Hewitt
Chamique Holdsclaw
Katie Holmes
Charlayne Hunter-Gault
Johanna Johnson
Craig Kielburger
John Lasseter
Peyton Manning
Ricky Martin
John McCain
Walter Payton
Freddie Prinze, Jr.
Viviana Risca
Briana Scurry
George Thampy
CeCe Winans

2001

Jessica Alba
Christiane Amanpour
Drew Barrymore
Jeff Bezos
Destiny's Child
Dale Earnhardt
Carly Fiorina
Aretha Franklin
Cathy Freeman
Tony Hawk
Faith Hill
Kim Dae-jung
Madeleine L'Engle
Mariangela Lisanti
Frankie Muniz
*N Sync
Ellen Ochoa
Jeff Probst
Julia Roberts
Carl T. Rowan
Britney Spears
Chris Tucker
Lloyd D. Ward
Alan Webb
Chris Weinke

2002

Aaliyah
Osama bin Laden
Mary J. Blige
Aubyn Burnside
Aaron Carter
Julz Chavez
Dick Cheney
Hilary Duff
Billy Gilman
Rudolph Giuliani
Brian Griese
Jennifer Lopez
Dave Mirra
Dineh Mohajer
Leanne Nakamura
Daniel Radcliffe
Condoleezza Rice
Marla Runyan
Ruth Simmons
Mattie Stepanek
J.R.R. Tolkien
Barry Watson
Tyrone Willingham
Elijah Wood

2003

Yolanda Adams
Olivia Bennett
Mildred Benson
Alexis Bledel
Barry Bonds
Vincent Brooks
Laura Bush
Amanda Bynes
Kelly Clarkson
Vin Diesel
Eminem
Michele Forman
Vicente Fox
Millard Fuller
Josh Hartnett
Dolores Huerta
Sarah Hughes
Enrique Iglesias
Jeanette Lee
John Lewis
Nicklas Lidstrom
Clint Mathis
Donovan McNabb

Nelly
Andy Roddick
Gwen Stefani
Emma Watson
Meg Whitman
Reese Witherspoon
Yao Ming

2004

Natalie Babbitt
David Beckham
Tony Blair
Kim Clijsters
Celia Cruz
Matel Dawson, Jr.
The Donnas
Tim Duncan
Shirin Ebadi
Ashton Kutcher
Lisa Leslie
Linkin Park
Irene D. Long
John Mayer
Mandy Moore
Thich Nhat Hanh
Raven
Keanu Reeves
Alexa Vega
Will Wright

Biography Today

Subject Series

Expands and complements the General Series and targets specific subject areas . . .

Our readers asked for it! They wanted more biographies, and the *Biography Today* **Subject Series** is our response to that demand. Now your readers can choose their special areas of interest and go on to read about their favorites in those fields. Priced at just $39 per volume, the following specific volumes are included in the *Biography Today* **Subject Series**:

- **Artists**
- **Authors**
- **Performing Artists**
- **Scientists & Inventors**
- **Sports**
- **World Leaders**
  Environmental Leaders
  Modern African Leaders

AUTHORS

"A useful tool for children's assignment needs." — *School Library Journal*

"The prose is workmanlike: report writers will find enough detail to begin sound investigations, and browsers are likely to find someone of interest." — *School Library Journal*

SCIENTISTS & INVENTORS

"The articles are readable, attractively laid out, and touch on important points that will suit assignment needs. Browsers will note the clear writing and interesting details."
— *School Library Journal*

"The book is excellent for demonstrating that scientists are real people with widely diverse backgrounds and personal interests. The biographies are fascinating to read."
— *The Science Teacher*

SPORTS

"This series should become a standard resource in libraries that serve intermediate students." — *School Library Journal*

ENVIRONMENTAL LEADERS #1

"A tremendous book that fills a gap in the biographical category of books. This is a great reference book." — *Science Scope*

FEATURES AND FORMAT

- Sturdy 6" x 9" hardbound volumes
- Individual volumes, $39 each
- 200 pages per volume
- 10 profiles per volume — targets individuals within a specific subject area
- Contact sources for additional information
- Cumulative General, Places of Birth, and Birthday Indexes

NOTE: There is *no duplication of entries* between the **General Series** of *Biography Today* and the **Subject Series**.

Artists

VOLUME 1

Ansel Adams
Romare Bearden
Margaret Bourke-White
Alexander Calder
Marc Chagall
Helen Frankenthaler
Jasper Johns
Jacob Lawrence
Henry Moore
Grandma Moses
Louise Nevelson
Georgia O'Keeffe
Gordon Parks
I.M. Pei
Diego Rivera
Norman Rockwell
Andy Warhol
Frank Lloyd Wright

Authors

VOLUME 1

Eric Carle
Alice Childress
Robert Cormier
Roald Dahl
Jim Davis
John Grisham
Virginia Hamilton
James Herriot
S.E. Hinton
M.E. Kerr
Stephen King
Gary Larson
Joan Lowery Nixon
Gary Paulsen
Cynthia Rylant
Mildred D. Taylor
Kurt Vonnegut, Jr.
E.B. White
Paul Zindel

VOLUME 2

James Baldwin
Stan and Jan Berenstain
David Macaulay
Patricia MacLachlan
Scott O'Dell
Jerry Pinkney
Jack Prelutsky

Lynn Reid Banks
Faith Ringgold
J.D. Salinger
Charles Schulz
Maurice Sendak
P.L. Travers
Garth Williams

VOLUME 3

Candy Dawson Boyd
Ray Bradbury
Gwendolyn Brooks
Ralph W. Ellison
Louise Fitzhugh
Jean Craighead George
E.L. Konigsburg
C.S. Lewis
Fredrick L. McKissack
Patricia C. McKissack
Katherine Paterson
Anne Rice
Shel Silverstein
Laura Ingalls Wilder

VOLUME 4

Betsy Byars
Chris Carter
Caroline B. Cooney
Christopher Paul Curtis
Anne Frank
Robert Heinlein
Marguerite Henry
Lois Lowry
Melissa Mathison
Bill Peet
August Wilson

VOLUME 5

Sharon Creech
Michael Crichton
Karen Cushman
Tomie dePaola
Lorraine Hansberry
Karen Hesse
Brian Jacques
Gary Soto
Richard Wright
Laurence Yep

VOLUME 6

Lloyd Alexander
Paula Danziger
Nancy Farmer
Zora Neale Hurston

Shirley Jackson
Angela Johnson
Jon Krakauer
Leo Lionni
Francine Pascal
Louis Sachar
Kevin Williamson

VOLUME 7

William H. Armstrong
Patricia Reilly Giff
Langston Hughes
Stan Lee
Julius Lester
Robert Pinsky
Todd Strasser
Jacqueline Woodson
Patricia C. Wrede
Jane Yolen

VOLUME 8

Amelia Atwater-Rhodes
Barbara Cooney
Paul Laurence Dunbar
Ursula K. Le Guin
Farley Mowat
Naomi Shihab Nye
Daniel Pinkwater
Beatrix Potter
Ann Rinaldi

VOLUME 9

Robb Armstrong
Cherie Bennett
Bruce Coville
Rosa Guy
Harper Lee
Irene Gut Opdyke
Philip Pullman
Jon Scieszka
Amy Tan
Joss Whedon

VOLUME 10

David Almond
Joan Bauer
Kate DiCamillo
Jack Gantos
Aaron McGruder
Richard Peck
Andrea Davis Pinkney
Louise Rennison
David Small
Katie Tarbox

VOLUME 11

Laurie Halse Anderson
Bryan Collier
Margaret Peterson
  Haddix
Milton Meltzer
William Sleator
Sonya Sones
Genndy Tartakovsky
Wendelin Van Draanen
Ruth White

VOLUME 12

An Na
Claude Brown
Meg Cabot
Virginia Hamilton
Chuck Jones
Robert Lipsyte
Lillian Morrison
Linda Sue Park
Pam Muñoz Ryan
Lemony Snicket
  (Daniel Handler)

VOLUME 13

Andrew Clements
Eoin Colfer
Sharon Flake
Edward Gorey
Francisco Jiménez
Astrid Lindgren
Chris Lynch
Marilyn Nelson
Tamora Pierce
Virginia Euwer Wolff

VOLUME 14

Orson Scott Card
Russell Freedman
Mary GrandPré
Dan Greenburg
Nikki Grimes
Laura Hillenbrand
Stephen Hillenburg
Norton Juster
Lurlene McDaniel
Stephanie S. Tolan

VOLUME 15

Liv Arnesen
Edward Bloor
Ann Brashares
Veronica Chambers
Mark Crilley
Paula Fox
Diana Wynne Jones
Victor Martinez
Robert McCloskey
Jerry Scott and Jim
    Borgman

Performing Artists

VOLUME 1

Jackie Chan
Dixie Chicks
Kirsten Dunst
Suzanne Farrell
Bernie Mac
Shakira
Isaac Stern
Julie Taymor
Usher
Christina Vidal

VOLUME 2

Ashanti
Tyra Banks
Peter Jackson
Norah Jones
Quincy Jones
Avril Lavigne
George López
Marcel Marceau
Eddie Murphy
Julia Stiles

VOLUME 3

Michelle Branch
Cameron Diaz
Missy Elliott
Evelyn Glennie
Benji Madden
Joel Madden
Mike Myers
Fred Rogers
Twyla Tharp
Tom Welling
Yuen Wo-Ping

Scientists & Inventors

VOLUME 1

John Bardeen
Sylvia Earle
Dian Fossey
Jane Goodall
Bernadine Healy
Jack Horner
Mathilde Krim
Edwin Land
Louise & Mary Leakey
Rita Levi-Montalcini
J. Robert Oppenheimer
Albert Sabin
Carl Sagan
James D. Watson

VOLUME 2

Jane Brody
Seymour Cray
Paul Erdös
Walter Gilbert
Stephen Jay Gould
Shirley Ann Jackson
Raymond Kurzweil
Shannon Lucid
Margaret Mead
Garrett Morgan
Bill Nye
Eloy Rodriguez
An Wang

VOLUME 3

Luis W. Alvarez
Hans A. Bethe
Gro Harlem Brundtland
Mary S. Calderone
Ioana Dumitriu
Temple Grandin
John Langston
    Gwaltney
Bernard Harris
Jerome Lemelson
Susan Love
Ruth Patrick
Oliver Sacks
Richie Stachowski

VOLUME 4

David Attenborough
Robert Ballard
Ben Carson
Eileen Collins
Biruté Galdikas
Lonnie Johnson
Meg Lowman
Forrest Mars Sr.
Akio Morita
Janese Swanson

VOLUME 5

Steve Case
Douglas Engelbart
Shawn Fanning
Sarah Flannery
Bill Gates
Laura Groppe
Grace Murray Hopper
Steven Jobs
Rand and Robyn Miller
Shigeru Miyamoto
Steve Wozniak

VOLUME 6

Hazel Barton
Alexa Canady
Arthur Caplan
Francis Collins
Gertrude Elion
Henry Heimlich
David Ho
Kenneth Kamler
Lucy Spelman
Lydia Villa-Komaroff

VOLUME 7

Tim Berners-Lee
France Córdova
Anthony S. Fauci
Sue Hendrickson
Steve Irwin
John Forbes Nash, Jr.
Jerri Nielsen
Ryan Patterson
Nina Vasan
Gloria WilderBrathwaite

VOLUME 8

Deborah Blum
Richard Carmona
Helene Gayle
Dave Kapell
Adriana C. Ocampo
John Romero
Jamie Rubin
Jill Tarter
Earl Warrick
Edward O. Wilson

VOLUME 9

Robert Barron
Regina Benjamin
Jim Cantore
Marion Donovan
Michael Fay
Laura L. Kiessling
Alvin Poussaint
Sandra Steingraber
Edward Teller
Peggy Whitson

Sports

VOLUME 1

Hank Aaron
Kareem Abdul-Jabbar
Hassiba Boulmerka
Susan Butcher
Beth Daniel
Chris Evert
Ken Griffey, Jr.
Florence Griffith Joyner
Grant Hill
Greg LeMond
Pelé
Uta Pippig
Cal Ripken, Jr.
Arantxa Sanchez
    Vicario
Deion Sanders
Tiger Woods

VOLUME 2

Muhammad Ali
Donovan Bailey
Gail Devers
John Elway
Brett Favre
Mia Hamm
Anfernee "Penny"
    Hardaway
Martina Hingis
Gordie Howe
Jack Nicklaus
Richard Petty
Dot Richardson
Sheryl Swoopes
Steve Yzerman

VOLUME 3

Joe Dumars
Jim Harbaugh
Dominik Hasek
Michelle Kwan
Rebecca Lobo
Greg Maddux
Fatuma Roba
Jackie Robinson
John Stockton
Picabo Street
Pat Summitt
Amy Van Dyken

VOLUME 4

Wilt Chamberlain
Brandi Chastain
Derek Jeter
Karch Kiraly
Alex Lowe
Randy Moss
Se Ri Pak
Dawn Riley
Karen Smyers
Kurt Warner
Serena Williams

VOLUME 5

Vince Carter
Lindsay Davenport
Lisa Fernandez
Fu Mingxia
Jaromir Jagr
Marion Jones
Pedro Martinez
Warren Sapp
Jenny Thompson
Karrie Webb

VOLUME 6

Jennifer Capriati
Stacy Dragila
Kevin Garnett
Eddie George
Alex Rodriguez
Joe Sakic
Annika Sorenstam
Jackie Stiles
Tiger Woods
Aliy Zirkle

VOLUME 7

Tom Brady
Tara Dakides
Alison Dunlap
Sergio Garcia
Allen Iverson
Shirley Muldowney
Ty Murray
Patrick Roy
Tasha Schwiker

VOLUME 8

Simon Ammann
Shannon Bahrke
Kelly Clark
Vonetta Flowers
Cammi Granato
Chris Klug
Jonny Moseley
Apolo Ohno
Sylke Otto
Ryne Sanborn
Jim Shea, Jr.

VOLUME 9

Tori Allen
Layne Beachley
Sue Bird
Fabiola da Silva
Randy Johnson
Jason Kidd
Tony Stewart
Michael Vick
Ted Williams
Jay Yelas

VOLUME 10

Ryan Boyle
Natalie Coughlin
Allyson Felix
Dallas Friday
Jean-Sébastien Giguère
Phil Jackson
Keyshawn Johnson
Tiffeny Milbrett
Alfonso Soriano
Diana Taurasi

World Leaders

VOLUME 1: Environmental Leaders 1

Edward Abbey
Renee Askins
David Brower
Rachel Carson
Marjory Stoneman Douglas
Dave Foreman
Lois Gibbs
Wangari Maathai
Chico Mendes
Russell A. Mittermeier
Margaret and Olaus J. Murie
Patsy Ruth Oliver
Roger Tory Peterson
Ken Saro-Wiwa
Paul Watson
Adam Werbach

VOLUME 2: Modern African Leaders

Mohammed Farah Aidid
Idi Amin
Hastings Kamuzu Banda
Haile Selassie
Hassan II
Kenneth Kaunda
Jomo Kenyatta
Winnie Mandela
Mobutu Sese Seko
Robert Mugabe
Kwame Nkrumah
Julius Kambarage Nyerere
Anwar Sadat
Jonas Savimbi
Léopold Sédar Senghor
William V. S. Tubman

VOLUME 3: Environmental Leaders 2

John Cronin
Dai Qing
Ka Hsaw Wa
Winona LaDuke
Aldo Leopold
Bernard Martin
Cynthia Moss
John Muir
Gaylord Nelson
Douglas Tompkins
Hazel Wolf